Thinking
and Acting
Like a
Solution–Focused
School
Counselor

For Bernadette Simpson and Michael Pillagalli, two people whose dedication, personal values, professional competence, and caring spirits have touched and shaped the lives of so many students.

RICHARD D. PARSONS

Thinking
and Acting
Like a
Solution-Focused
School
Counselor

CORWIN
A SAGE Company

For information:

Corwin
A SAGE Company
2455 Teller Road
Thousand Oaks, California 91320
(800) 233-9936
Fax: (800) 417-2466
www.corwinpress.com

SAGE India Pvt. Ltd.
B 1/I 1 Mohan Cooperative
   Industrial Area
Mathura Road, New Delhi 110 044
India

SAGE Ltd.
1 Oliver's Yard
55 City Road
London EC1Y 1SP
United Kingdom

SAGE Asia-Pacific Pte. Ltd.
33 Pekin Street #02-01
Far East Square
Singapore 048763

Printed in the United States of America.

Library of Congress Cataloging-in-Publication Data

Parsons, Richard D.
Thinking and acting like a solution-focused school counselor / Richard D. Parsons.
      p. cm.
Includes bibliographical references and index.
ISBN 978-1-4129-6644-3 (cloth)
ISBN 978-1-4129-6645-0 (pbk.)
    1. Educational counseling—Vocational guidance. 2. Solution-focused therapy for children. I. Title.

LB1027.5.P3197 2009
371.4′25—dc22   2009010942

This book is printed on acid-free paper.

09   10   11   12   13   10   9   8   7   6   5   4   3   2   1

Acquisitions Editor:	Arnis Burvikovs
Associate Editor:	Desirée A. Bartlett
Production Editor:	Eric Garner
Copy Editor:	Gretchen Treadwell
Typesetter:	C&M Digitals (P) Ltd.
Proofreader:	Carole Quandt
Indexer:	Jean Casalegno
Cover Designer:	Michael Dubowe

Contents

Preface

School Counseling From a Solution-Focused Perspective

*T*hinking and Acting Like a Solution-Focused School Counselor provides an in-depth look at the impact of employing a solution-focused perspective on one's counseling decisions and practice. The book presents the underlying philosophy, fundamental constructs, and concepts that take form in the specific intervention strategies employed by the solution-focused school counselor. However, the unique value of *Thinking and Acting Like a Solution-Focused School Counselor* is that it goes beyond the presentation of a theory and assists the readers to step into that theory, embrace it as an organizational framework and then—and most importantly—employ it to guide their procedural thinking when confronted with student information.

TEXT FORMAT AND CHAPTER STRUCTURE

Research suggests that procedural knowledge—that is, knowing what to do when the student does this or that—is acquired as the result of practice accompanied by feedback. As such, *practice and feedback are central to this text.* Case illustrations, and case presentations with analyses of counselor actions and the decision-making processes underlying them, along with guided-practice activities, will be employed as "teaching tools" throughout the text.

The effective use of procedural knowledge is a hallmark of expert counselors. It is my hope that this book facilitates your own development of procedural knowledge and in so doing, supports you and your valued work of counseling our children.

—RDP

Acknowledgments

While I have been credited with the authorship of this text, many others have significantly contributed to the formation and shaping of my thoughts into the text you hold in your hands. First, I want to thank Arnis Burvikovs at Corwin for encouraging me to pursue this book series. I would like to acknowledge the support and encouragement I have received from my colleagues, particularly Naijian Zhang, Wally Kahn, and Charles Good. I sincerely appreciate the hard work and editorial support provided me by my graduate assistant, Erica Morrison, as well as the fine work of Gretchen Treadwell. Finally, I would like to publicly thank my wife, Ginny, not only for her professional insights but also for ongoing affirmation and support.

—RDP

Corwin gratefully acknowledges the contributions of the following individuals:

Sharie Blankenship, School Counselor
Ardmore City Schools
Ardmore, OK

Jill R. Boyd, Counselor and Olweus Bullying Prevention Trainer
John Bullen Middle School
Kenosha, WI

Stuart F. Chen-Hayes, Program Coordinator
Counselor Education and School Counseling
Lehman College, City University of New York
Bronx, NY

Gloria Avolio DePaul, School Counselor
School District of Hillsborough County
Tampa, FL

Karen M. Joseph, School Counseling Department Director
Roberto Clemente Middle School
Germantown, MD

Cynthia Knowles, Prevention Specialist
Livonia Central School District
Livonia, NY

William Livers, School Social Worker
SW Parke Community Schools District
Montezuma, IN

Andy Mennick, High School Guidance/College Counselor
The American International School of Bucharest
Bucharest, Romania

Marcy F. Pellegrini, Counselor
Los Angeles Unified School District
Van Nuys, CA

Victoria Poedubicky, School Counselor
Bartle Elementary School
Highland Park, NJ

Diane Smith, School Counselor
Smethport Area School District
Smethport, PA

Joyce Stout, Elementary School Counselor
Redondo Beach Unified School District
Redondo Beach, CA

Zulema I. Suarez, School Counselor
Tucson Unified School District
Tucson, AZ

Kay Herting Wahl, Director of School Counseling
Clinical Training Director
University of Minnesota
Minneapolis, MN

About the Author

Richard D. Parsons, PhD, is a full professor in the Department of Counseling and Educational Psychology at West Chester University in Eastern Pennsylvania. Dr. Parsons has over thirty-two years of university teaching in counselor preparation programs. Prior to his university teaching, Dr. Parsons spent nine years as a school counselor in an inner-city high school. Dr. Parsons has been the recipient of many awards and honors, including the Pennsylvania Counselor of the Year award.

Dr. Parsons has authored or coauthored over eighty professional articles and books. His most recent books include the texts: *Counseling Strategies That Work! Evidenced-Based for School Counselors* (2006), *The School Counselor as Consultant* (2004), *Teacher as Reflective Practitioner and Action Researcher* (2001), *Educational Psychology* (2001), *The Ethics of Professional Practice* (2000), *Counseling Strategies and Intervention Techniques* (1994), and *The Skills of Helping* (1995). In addition to these texts, Dr. Parsons has authored or coauthored three seminal works in the area of psycho-educational consultation, *Mental Health Consultation in the Schools* (1993), *Developing Consultation Skills* (1985), and *The Skilled Consultant* (1995).

Dr. Parsons has a private practice and serves as a consultant to educational institutions and mental health service organizations throughout the tri-state area. Dr. Parsons has served as a national consultant to the Council of Independent Colleges in Washington, DC, providing institutions of higher education with assistance in the areas of program development, student support services, pedagogical innovation and assessment procedures.

Introduction to Book Series

Transforming Theory Into Practice

There was a time—at least this is what I've been told—when school counselors were called upon to calm the child who lost his lunch, intervene with two middle school students who were "name-calling," and provide guidance to a senior considering college options. Now, I know these tasks are still on school counselors' "things-to-do lists," but a brief review of any one typical day in the life of a school counselor will suggest that these were the good old days!

You do not need the research or statistics on divorce rates, violence, drug use, sexual abuse, etc. to "know" that our society and our children are in crises. Each of the multitude of referrals you receive provides you with abundant evidence of this crisis.

It is not just the increased number of children seeking your assistance that is the issue—it is the increased severity and complexity of problems with which they present. The problems addressed by today's school counselor certainly include "name calling" and teasing, but sadly, in today's society, that form of interaction can quickly escalate to violence involving deadly weapons. Perhaps you still have the child or two who is upset about misplaced lunches—or homework, or jackets—but it is also not unusual to find the upset is grounded in the anticipated abuse that will be received when his or her parent finds out.

School children with significant depression, debilitating anxieties, energy-draining obsessions, damaged self-concepts, and self-destructive behaviors can be found in any school and in any counselor's office throughout our land. Responding to these children in ways that facilitate their development and foster their growth through education is a daunting task for today's school counselor. It is a task that demands a high degree of knowledge, skill, and competency. It is a task that demands effective, efficient translation of theory and research into practice.

The current series, *Transforming Theory Into Practice,* provides school counselors practical guides to gathering and processing client data, developing case conceptualizations, and formulating and implementing specific treatment plans. Each book in the series emphasizes skill development and, as such, each book provides extensive case illustrations and guided-practice exercises in order to move the reader from simply "knowing" to "doing."

The expanding needs of our children, along with the demands for increased accountability in our profession, require that each of us continue to sharpen our knowledge and skills as helping professionals. It is the hope that the books presented within this series, *Transforming Theory Into Practice,* facilitate your own professional development and support you in your valued work of counseling our children.

Part I

Solution Focus: A Model Guiding Reflective Practice

Solution-focused theory, while intellectually interesting, remains just that—a theory—until it is translated into practice. For the school counselor, the real value of a counseling theory or model is in its potential to facilitate the process of gathering student information, discerning what is important from what is not, and knowing what needs to be done to move the student from the "what is" to the "what is desired." The information found within Part I emphasizes the value of a solution-focused model for the reflective practice of the school counselor. Chapter 1 introduces the reader to the concept of reflective practice as a process shaping the decisions and actions of the effective school counselor. Chapter 2 outlines the fundamental principles and constructs of a solution-focused approach to school counseling as a valuable orientating framework to guide this reflective practice.

The School Counselor as Reflective Practitioner

1

"I hate my life! Nobody likes me. My mother will kill me 'cause I'm failing everything and I look like a fat pig."

The above was the "greeting" the counselor received as he sat down to speak with a tearful eighth grader named Katie.[1] Perhaps as you read the above quote, you began to generate a number of "hypotheses" about what may be going on, as well as what you, as a counselor, would need to do.

While trained to be good listeners, school counselors understand that listening is but the vehicle to understanding, and that understanding is the base from which we formulate our helping strategies. The current chapter presents school counseling as a reflective practice. The reflective school counselor gathers student data and employs those data to shape and adjust his or her treatment plans and guide moment-to-moment counseling interactions.

COUNSELORS IN SEARCH OF MEANING

In the course of any one day, school counselors may engage with students whose stories are often unclear, complicated, and even convoluted. In the privacy of their offices or in the brief encounters in the hallways, effective school counselors are able to move quickly beyond listening, and attending to understanding the "real" story embedded in the students' words and actions.

A simple statement such as, "Hi, can I talk with you?" or "My teacher sent me down," are actually invitations to the school counselor to engage in a search for meaning. The effective counselor responds to this invitation by eliciting the student's story while at the same time attempting to (1) discern what is important from what is not, (2) understand the "what is" and the 'what is hoped for," and (3) develop connections that will guide the student to this desired outcome.

A counselor working with Katie may, for example, attempt to discern the depth of Katie's "hatred." Was this a preamble to suicidal ideation and action? Or was it simply the adolescent's dramatic response to a momentary "crisis"? Perhaps the counselor working with Katie may confront the validity of her conclusions regarding the absence of friendship or the failing of "everything." Or, perhaps the counselor relying on previous knowledge and experience working with Katie may interpret her response as simply one reflecting the melodrama of a "typical" teen. With this latter interpretation, the counselor may feel no need to test for suicidal ideation, or confront the reality of her conclusions, but rather simply recognize the value of providing an attending and supportive ear. But which direction should the counselor take? How should the counselor understand Katie's disclosures?

The effective school counselor certainly listens to a student's story—but does so with a discerning ear in search of meaning. Listening to students' disclosures and attempting to make meaning of those disclosures requires that a school counselor employ a model, a guide, and an orienting framework that places these disclosures into some meaningful context. The current text focuses upon the use of a *solution-focused* orienting framework to guide this discernment, this search for meaning. However, prior to getting into the theory and its application to school counseling, it is important to first highlight the value of a reflective process for all counselors, regardless of theoretical orientation.

COUNSELOR REFLECTIONS
GUIDING PRACTICE DECISIONS

The counselor's ability to reflect on his or her counseling has been identified as an essential component to effective practice (Nelson & Neufeldt, 1998). This reflection provides the counselor the means to make sense of all the data presented by a student and to connect those data with a specific counselor response both at the macrolevel of treatment planning and at the microlevel of moment-to-moment interaction that occurs within a session.

Reflection at the Macrolevel:
Case Conceptualization and Treatment Planning

It is clear that not all student information is of equal value or importance to the process and outcome of the counseling. Using an orienting framework, such as the solution-focused model, the school counselor reflects on the student's disclosures and formulates these data into a coherent, yet tentative, conceptualization of what is, what is desired, and how to move from "A" to "B."

This ability to conceptualize "what is" in terms of presenting concerns and student's resources, and the "what is hoped for," that is, the goals and outcomes for the counseling, sets the framework for consideration of strategies and techniques needed to move the student toward the desired outcome. With this conceptualization in mind, the counselor will call upon previous experience as well as knowledge of current research to begin selecting the strategies to employ.

This reflection and planning is not a static, one-time process—rather, it refers to the thinking that takes place following a session or an encounter that allows the counselor to review what he or she did, what he or she anticipated would happen, and what in fact did happen. Taking time to reflect upon and consider the "experience" of the session helps provide data from which to judge the direction the sessions are taking, determine the rate that the student is moving in the desired direction, and even helps the counselor develop a set of questions, ideas, and propositions to be tested in the next encounter. This reflection on practice allows the counselor to refine the case conceptualization and reframe the direction of the strategies employed. This process of reflection "on" practice is depicted in Figure1.1, and further illustrated by the following case.

Rick, a bright, successful, and well-liked eleventh-grade student came to counseling seeking assistance with his college selection process. Having served as Rick's counselor since his entrance into the school in ninth-grade, Mr. "P" felt that he had a good handle on Rick and had established an excellent working relationship. With these historic data as his bases, Mr. P approached the session with the intent of directing Rick to the self-search program as an initial step to identifying a pool of colleges of interest (*Step 1: Identification of goal [or subgoal]*). In preparing to develop a treatment plan, the counselor relied on two sources of knowledge (*Step 2: Review of knowledge base/experience*):

a. A review of Rick's cumulative folder revealed that he was an honor student; successful athlete lettering in both varsity basketball and football; and a star socially, being class president and voted

Figure 1.1   Reflection "on" Practice

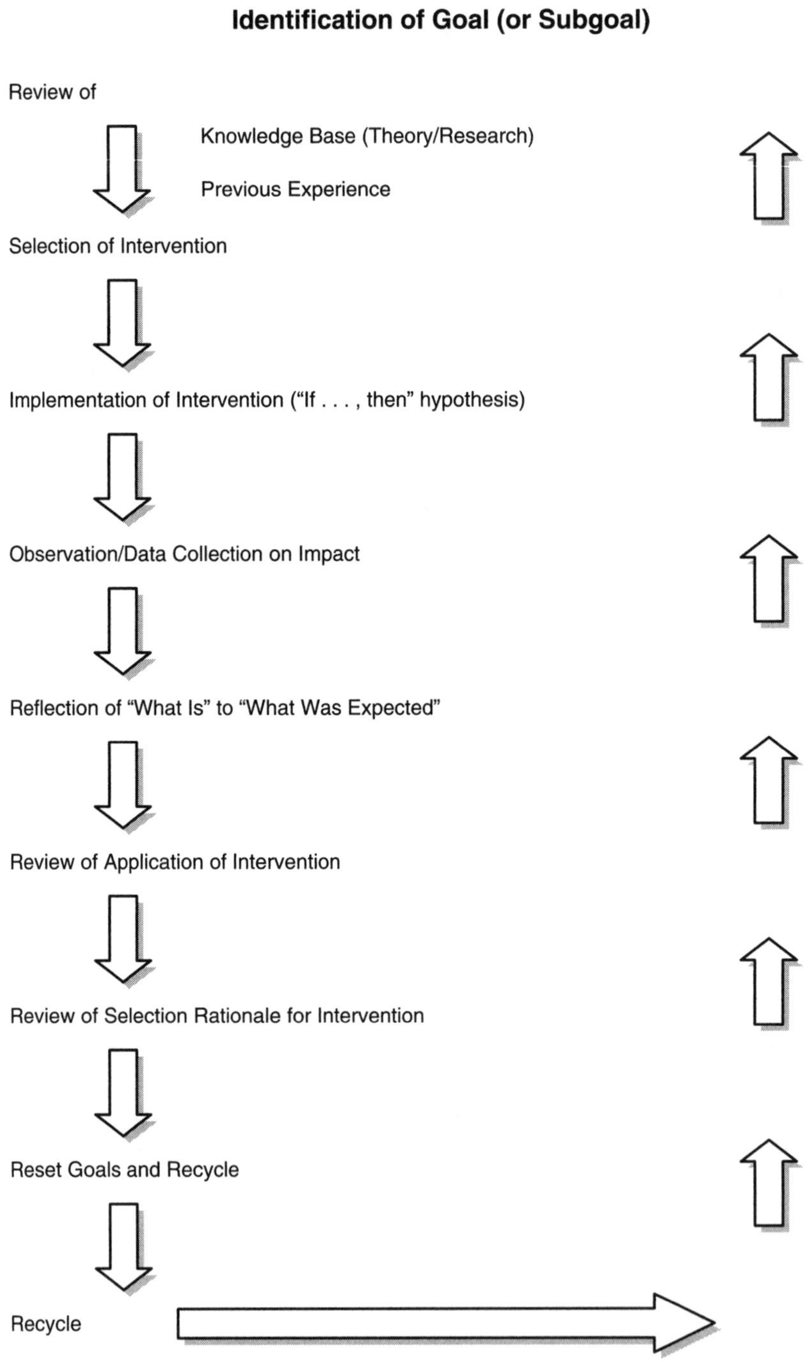

Identification of Goal (or Subgoal)

Review of

⬇   Knowledge Base (Theory/Research)

           Previous Experience

Selection of Intervention

⬇   ⬆

Implementation of Intervention ("If . . . , then" hypothesis)

⬇   ⬆

Observation/Data Collection on Impact

⬇   ⬆

Reflection of "What Is" to "What Was Expected"

⬇   ⬆

Review of Application of Intervention

⬇   ⬆

Review of Selection Rationale for Intervention

⬇   ⬆

Reset Goals and Recycle

⬇   ⬆

Recycle   ➡

"homecoming king." Rick's mom and dad were both successful professionals (mom a physician and dad CEO for a financial company) and were very supportive of Rick, their eldest son.

b. Prior to meeting with Rick, Mr. P reviewed Rick's interest inventory, noting that he had consistently expressed an interest in medicine and, as such, Mr. P researched universities with good track records placing students into medical schools

With this information as the knowledge base, Mr. P proposed that Rick start with a listing of highly competitive and competitive schools, and with the aid of the computerized self-search program, review university descriptions, requirements, etc. (*Step 3: Select intervention*). The plan was enacted using the following steps (*Step 4: Intervention implementation*):

a. First, Mr. P explained the search process.

b. Rick sat and simply "played" with program options as Mr. P provided instruction and support.

c. Once comfortable with the program, Rick would use his study hall over the course of the next two weeks to begin to identify universities "of interest," which he and Mr. P. would review, together.

Both Mr. P and Rick felt good about the program and thus, it was implemented. Over the course of the next couple of days, Rick would come to the counseling office during his study period and, after saying hi to Mr. P., would proceed to the career center and the self-directed search. Early in the second week, when Rick stopped in, Mr. P greeted him and asked how it was going. Rick's response, while stating "okay," was couched in a tone and body language that suggested it was anything but okay! (*Step 4: Observation and data collection.*)

While Mr. P had anticipated that by this point in the process, Rick would be getting excited about his finds, the lack of enthusiasm was significant (*Step 5: Comparison of "what is" to "what was expected"*). Sitting with Rick, it was clear he had no problem using the self-directed search and in fact was able to read about a variety of university programs; thus, the initial "intervention" was implemented (*Step 6: Review of application*) and it should have worked, given the counselor's experience and the extensive supportive research (*Step 7: Review rationale*). The question of course is, "Why wasn't it?" Why wasn't he becoming excited and more focused on specific programs? (*Step 8: Reset goals and recycle.*)

As a result of meeting with Rick and asking him about his experience, it became clear that finding a specific college of choice was *not* the desired goal. Rather, Rick began to share that he really wasn't sure that he wanted to go to college right after graduation, but felt that this would devastate his parents and subsequently was becoming increasingly anxious and depressed about having to do something he truly did not want to do. As evidenced by this case illustration, an essential component to our reflection "on" practice is our awareness of movement toward desired outcome. Reflecting "on" these new data resulted in the resetting of the goals of counseling and the interventions to be employed.

Ridley (1995) stated that many counselors assume that their good intentions make them helpful clinicians. This oftentimes gets translated into the "it felt good" approach to counseling in which as long as the student appeared to "enjoy" the exchange, then a positive outcome could be assumed. This assumption can lead to the use of bad, although well intended, interventions. To avoid the good intentions-bad interventions scenario, Ridley (1995) urged counselors to evaluate the effectiveness of their interventions regarding their helpfulness. This is the crux of reflection "on" practice.

While some school counselors may attempt to use formal assessment tools to assess movement toward outcome, valuable reflection can be guided by consideration of questions such as:

1. What is my formulation of the problem or issue of concern?

2. What specific student factors (readiness, motivation, levels of awareness, specific resources, etc.) do I need to consider?

3. Do I have enough information to start the case conceptualization and treatment planning? What else do I need to know?

4. What is the strength of my relationship with the student? Has our history been positive? Can I move to the work of change or do I need to continue to develop a facilitating relationship? Is the relationship supportive of student disclosure and reception to feedback? What other factors or elements significant to a helping relationship are present? Absent?

5. Given my knowledge, experience, and competency, how best can I assist this student? Do I serve as treatment provider? Is referral-out required? What is my role now and in the future with this student?

6. What are my goals for the next session? How do I proceed? How will I assess the progress of the next session?

School counselors who take time to reflect on practice are more aware of what they did and why they did it. The effective counselor uses this reflection to not only assess the degree of movement toward the desired goal, but also to serve as the bases from which to make adjustments to the plan and thus increase his or her effectiveness.

Reflection at the Microlevel: Reflection "in" Process

While it is essential to use student data for case conceptualization and intervention planning, school counselors know that counseling is a dynamic process and cannot be staged in nice linear steps. School counselors appreciate that while they may be prepared with a well-thought plan and a well-stocked "intervention toolbox," these cannot simply be applied in a one-size-fits-all approach to counseling. The subtleties of each relationship, the unique characteristics of both participants, and the context of time and place all contribute to the need for counselors to fine-tune and adjust these plans, and often devise strategies right at the moment of interaction.

The effective counselor not only reflects on his or her counseling outside of the session, but does so while in the process of interacting with a student, within any one session. Approaching the situation as a reflective conversation, the expert school counselor views each exchange—each moment of interaction—as an intervention, an intervention that needs to be observed and assessed for effectiveness. Thus, counselors reflecting in process are simultaneously involved in design and implementation of action, "[. . .] while at the same time remaining detached enough to observe and feel the action that is occurring, and to respond" (Tremmel, 1993, p. 436). Consider the simple example of offering a tissue to a tearful student. What is the intent of such a gesture? While such a gesture appears perhaps caring and helpful, might it signal that tears are not allowed? Could offering the tissue highlight and thus sensitize a student who feels somewhat embarrassed by the tears? Is this the purpose of the activity?

The reflective counselor knows what he or she expected to achieve by this gesture and will rapidly process the student's reactions, contrasting it to what was expected, and adjust accordingly. Therefore, the counselor who is providing the tissue as an invitation to share feelings may note the student's dismissal of that invitation and, in turn, simply state, "Ginny, you seem upset. Would you like to tell me what's going on?" Or, perhaps the counselor offers the tissues as a simple physical comfort, but notes that the client becomes embarrassed by the counselor's recognition of the apparent upset. Under these conditions, the counselor may simply lower the box and place it on the table, redirecting the student with the comment, "Ginny, I'm glad you are here. Have a seat (pointing to a chair) and make yourself comfortable." These are not actions that can be prescribed nor even anticipated, but require the rapid processing of data and comparison of *what is* to *what was hoped for*, with the end result being an adjustment of counselor action.

ORIENTING FRAMEWORKS GUIDING REFLECTION

In order for the counselor's reflections to result in meaningful adjustment in counselor style or interventions, the counselor needs to be aware of the disparity between what is and what was expected. But how does a counselor know what to expect? What are the standards, the measures, against which to contrast actual events to expected events and outcomes? It is in answering these questions that one's orienting framework or counseling model comes to play.

Our counseling models not only place the student's issues within a meaningful context, but also establish what to expect when stimuli for change are introduced (Irving & Williams, 1995). Without such an orienting framework or theory, we truly can become "directionless creatures bombarded with literally hundreds of impressions and pieces of information in a single session" (Procaska & Norcross, 1994, p. 3).

The remainder of this book is devoted to the presentation of one such orienting framework, *solution-focused counseling*. In the chapters to follow, not only will the tenants of a solution-focused model to school counseling be presented, but also the value of this orienting framework as a guide to reflective practice will be illustrated.

SUMMARY

Counselors in Search of Meaning

- Listening to student disclosure, and attempting to make meaning of those disclosures, requires that a school counselor employ a model, a guide, and an orienting framework to place these disclosures into some meaningful context.

Counselor Reflections Guiding Practice Decisions

- The counselor's ability to reflect on his or her counseling has been identified as an essential component of effective practice.

- Reflection provides the counselor the means to make sense of all the data presented by a student and to connect those data with a counselor response and interventions.

Orienting Frameworks Guiding Reflection

- A counselor's theory, model, or orienting framework provides the "structure" needed to begin to understand the large amount of information gathered in counseling and that understanding is used to formulate effective intervention plans.

NOTE

1. All client names and reference materials reflect composite cases and not a single actual student.

The Fundamentals 2
of a Solution-
Focused Organizing
Framework

S olution-focused brief therapy first appeared in the early1980s. The title
and the development of the specific steps of solution-focused brief
therapy have been attributed to Steve de Shazer and his wife Insoo Kim Berg,
and their team at the Brief Family Therapy Family Center in Milwaukee,
Wisconsin. The solution-focused model represents a significant departure
from the more classic problem-focused therapeutic approaches. It is a
departure that is ideally suited for use by school counselors (Sklare, 1997).

School counselors employing a solution-focused orienting framework
approach their work with students by highlighting students' strengths
and assets, opposed to hunting for weaknesses and disability. The
solution-focused school counselor emphasizes the positive with a focus
on the achievement of future goals, opposed to investing time and energy
in remediation of past mistakes. School counselors viewing data through
the lens of the solution-focused model see students not as coming to
counseling seeking solutions to their problems, but rather as individuals
with solutions seeking expression. This shift in focus has a huge impact on
how the counselor views his or her own role, the role of the student, what
is important and meaningful, and the steps to employ to facilitate
movement toward articulated goals.

The solution-focused counselor takes an active role—"conducting"
the counseling—and takes responsibility for unfolding the helping
process. While shaping the process, the solution-focused school counselor
develops a collaborative relationship with students and together they
establish goals, find solutions, and incorporate solution processes that

lead to goal achievement. Rather than fault finding and extensive review of problems and difficulties, the solution-focused school counselor engages the student in conversation about goals and existing resources that can be used to move the student in the desired direction. This goal-oriented focus along with the emphasis on positives in the student's life can be a welcome relief to the student who often feels beat up by adult criticism, and who is in real need of hope.

MORE THAN JUST NEW TECHNIQUES: A NEW PERSPECTIVE

The first step to becoming a solution-focused counselor is to change our thinking (Nelson & Neufeldt, 1998). A solution-focused approach to school counseling entails much more than simply employing specific strategies and techniques; it is more than new techniques—it is truly a new perspective. For school counselors to effectively employ a solution-focused model through which to filter student data, make meaning, and in turn create interventions, they will need to embrace a new worldview provided by this model. It is a worldview that incorporates each of the following.

A Constructivist Philosophy

The solution-focused model has been aligned with a constructivist philosophy (O'Connell, 1998). This philosophy posits that we do not have direct access to objective truth and reality; rather, we are dependent on our linguistically constructed versions of reality. Once created and conveyed, these concepts, labels, and verbal descriptions are empowered through social relationships and interactions and, once assimilated, create realities within the individual. Consider the impact on the experienced realities of those who are gay when the American Psychiatric Association removed homosexuality from its classification of psychiatric disorder. For some homosexuals, the very process of embracing the social definition of their orientation as ill, sick, or even sinful resulted in their experience of anxiety, depression, and even self-loathing. However, the very process of redefining homosexuality as no longer a pathology not only removed this category from a reference book, but reinforced a social construct which defines gay as different not sick, nor ill. Embracing homosexuality as simply a different sexual orientation and not a pathological one leads to significant psycho-emotional changes and self-perceptions for those who are homosexual. Such is the power of constructivism.

School counselors are aware of the self-fulfilling prophecy concept. It too can be viewed as a reflection of the power of constructivism. If we expect one to act out and we convey that to the individual over and over until he or she embraces it as reality, then acting out in line with the "reality" seems a logical conclusion. This is a very powerful concept and has many implications for the school counselor and the approach to working with students. Do we approach children as if they have problems or are a problem? Would it make a difference? Do we invite students to discuss, reflect, maybe even analyze all their limitations, weaknesses, and histories of failure, or do we focus on the future, goals, and the resources the student has that can lead to this desired future? Again, does it—would it—make a difference? Those employing a solution-focused orienting framework believe so and have their actions guided by that belief.

The counselor operating from a constructivism point of view posits that the language employed in counseling coconstructs problems and solutions, thus creating reality rather than merely reflecting it. Thus, a counselor confronted with a student who has been disruptive and acting out in class might ask, "Why do you do that?" or more strongly, "What's wrong with you?" The solution-focused counselor would appreciate the power of language and constructed realities and thus not use language of blame or problem focus, but rather invite the student to consider how he or she would like to be different. With this lens, the counselor might ask, "How would you like it to be different in class?" Such a question would quickly be followed by discussion around issues and solutions—getting there—rather than focus on problems and how we got here. By focusing the encounter on solutions and hopeful futures, as opposed to becoming mired in a discussion of the student's unsuccessful and problematic history, a reality of hope and positive expectations is created. Finally and perhaps most importantly, embracing a constructionist point of view positions the solution-focused school counselor to approach student problems as neither fixed, nor immutable truths, but rather as constructed realities that can be changed.

What's So Different?

As previously suggested, in order to be truly effective, the school counselor needs to not only employ strategies derived from this model, but also embrace and assimilate the philosophy and fundamental principles underlying these strategies. While this process may, at first blush, appear simple enough for those of us trained in traditional models and theories of counseling, it may in fact be quite a challenge.

For most school counselors, embracing a solution-focused orienting framework will represent a major paradigm shift. The solution-focused school counselor uses problem-free language and shifts his or her focus away from problems, causes, and pathology to goals and successes

(George, Iveson, & Ratner, 1999). Making this shift is not easy. Moving to goals and solutions and resisting the tendency to seek that which is broke can be difficult for those school counselors trained in traditional counseling theory. The shift is encompassing and takes form in even the most subtle elements of our interactions as we avoid "problem speak."

As an illustration of the extent to which this is truly a shift in paradigm, consider the simple process of greeting a student who comes to the counselor's office. The student—either self or other referred—may come to the office showing some sign of concern or upset. As the student enters the office, it would not be unusual to hear the counselor invite the student to share his or her concern—identify and describe the problem—and continue to investigate, in depth, the various forms and history of this dilemma. The simple step of asking the student, "What's wrong?" or "What happened?" sets the stage for focusing on problems, failures, faults, and deficits. Certainly, such a response would be appropriately reactive to the child in distress, but from a constructivist perspective, it also sets up the "reality" that there is a problem and that the student is there in need of help in order to right this wrong. For the solution-focused counselor, such a constructed reality is counterproductive.

Contrast this simple introduction to that offered by the solution-focused counselor who, while comforting the child, asks, "What can we do to make this better?" or "What do you hope we can do that would make coming here worthwhile?" While the student may have difficulty providing an answer to these or similar goal-focused questions, the questions serve the purpose of reframing the encounter as one that is and will be positive and goal directed. Inviting the student to consider what it is he or she would like to achieve by coming to the counselor frames the issue as future and goal oriented, and does so in a way that reflects a hopefulness about the encounter. The elimination of "problem speak" is a subtle, yet significant difference between a more traditional problem-focused model and that of solution focus. It is in the subtlety that we find the meaningful difference. It is a difference that reflects a true paradigmatic shift as highlighted in Table 2.1.

Problem Students, or Problematic Experiences?

The solution-focused counselor doesn't deny the existence of a problem, but recognizes that the problem is the problem and not the student. Sadly, it is not unusual to overhear a discussion about a student in which the person of the student is discussed in negative, if not, pathological terms. Perhaps it is a statement about a child who is really a "pain," or "bad," or a real "failure," or maybe the label is somewhat more clinical and

Table 2.1 Targets for Reflective Practice: Intake

Solution-Focused Orienting Framework	Traditional/Classical Approach to Counseling
Establish a collaborative, cooperative, customer-based relationship.	Establish rapport and a trusting working alliance.
Identify student's desired outcome for the counseling process.	Identify and define the nature of the problem.
Identify impact on day-to-day life experience if student achieves desired goals.	Explore the depth and breadth of the problem.
Identify "exceptions" to the problem experience. When in the past has the student experienced some of the desired goal and how did he or she do that?	Identify strategies employed in the past—identifying those that have not worked.
Identify what one small step would look like and what it would take to move in that direction.	Set the stage for the application of a best-practice intervention plan.

the student is referred to as hyperactive or depressed or psychopathic! In each of these situations, it is the person of the student that is labeled as faulty. It is not a student who is experiencing depression or encountering difficulty sitting still or at times breaks the rules. No, the language too often used is that which defines the person—the student—as a problem. Under these conditions, the "what to do" appears almost hopeless, for how are we, as school counselors, to change the person of the student?

For the solution-focused school counselor, "problems" are not indications of something fundamentally wrong with the student, they simply are experiences that occur in the natural flow of human interaction. They are times when the student experiences a block or disruption in the way he or she would like his or her life to be. With this reframe, the solution-focused counselor's interests and attentions are drawn to the identification and clarification of preferred scenarios, rather than an analysis of the current, less desired state. Another outcome of this perspective of viewing the student as experiencing a problem, rather than a problematic student, is that the solution-focused counselor expects that the problem—while existing at this time and within this context—is not fixed and totally pervasive throughout the student's life. The belief is that there are times and situations in which this student is not experiencing this problem. There are times and situations when the student has and does experience success. Given this belief, the solution-focused counselor is less interested in unearthing or discovering the cause of the student's problem, and more interested in investigating those times of success—those exceptions to the current situation.

Knowing how the student succeeds, and has either avoided or reduced problems at other times or in other circumstances, gives insight and direction for what could be done at this moment to return the student to a goal-oriented path. Rather than seeking direction in the research or in articulated formal intervention strategies as would be typical for counselors operating from a traditional counseling model, the solution-focused school counselor looks to the student as the resource. Valuing the wealth of resources that each student brings to the relationship, the solution-focused school counselor seeks to understand how solutions have occurred in the past (exceptions) and how the student may use these to make for a different future. For example, the same student who experiences difficulty paying attention in class may have a wealth of successful experiences attending to video games. Or, the student who reacts negatively to a peer's in-class taunt is the same student who is able to ignore the "trash talk" of a member of the opposing team during a basketball game in which he is engaged.

The solution-focused school counselor sees these experiences as invaluable resources to crafting strategies to allow that student to respond similarly within the classroom. Valuing the student for having the essential resources needed for goal achievement elevates the student into a role of collaborator rather than a "client" in need of help! In this framework, the solutions are collaboratively constructed, rather than created and proclaimed by the "expert helper."

FUNDAMENTAL PRINCIPLES
GUIDING SOLUTION-FOCUSED PRACTICE

School counselors employing these more traditional approaches to counseling as the lens through which to process student information would employ strategies that facilitated: (1) the development of the therapeutic relationship, (2) an elaborate articulation of the student's problems or concerns, (3) the determination of problem genesis, and (4) the provision of increased insight or development of new cognitions or skills that would eliminate the problem. Contrast these more "traditional" targets and principles to those followed and employed by school counselors employing a solution-focused model.

Using of "Problem-Free" Talk

The solution-focused counselor, as a constructivist, posits language as playing an important role in how we perceive ourselves and the world around us. A major "task" for the solution-focused school counselor is to help students reframe their stories, their lived experiences, in a positive way so that they see themselves as more competent and their future more hopeful. To do this may require "redescribing" their concerns using language emphasizing solutions rather than problems (Metcalf, 1995). The following exchange provides an illustration of such "redescribing."

Jessica:	So, it seems that no matter how hard I try I still can't get it right.
Counselor:	Wow. That sounds frustrating. You really try hard and yet you still fail the test every time?
Jessica:	Yeah. Look here are my last three tests. I really studied for each one of these and for the last one I even got a study partner. She got an A and I got a C.
Counselor:	Jessica, I'm really impressed. How did you do that?
	(Redescribing)
Jessica:	Do what? Get a C?
Counselor:	Well, I guess that . . . since you failed the other tests . . . but I was really referring to the way you motivated yourself to keep at it. You know some people may give up but you really came up with a neat idea, getting a study buddy.
Jessica:	Yeah, I don't know. I just felt like "I can do this" and Linda gets really good grades so I figured why not ask her.
Counselor:	I think that is super! I wonder, if we looked at what you and Linda did that was different than the way you studied before, if we could discover something we could use for the next test?

The counselor illustrated in this brief exchange clearly listened for evidence of Jessica's strengths. Having identified Jessica's strong motivation and creativity, the counselor redescribed the situation as one that was an investigation of what worked, rather than a retelling of failure and a pursuit of fault. The counselor avoided problem speak and began to refocus the dialogue to solution focus.

Reframing and realistically redescribing these situations helps the students feel less damaged and defensive, and more hopeful and receptive to the counseling.

Redescribing the situation as an investigation of what works helps to not only reduce the student's defensiveness, but will also result in meaningful data from which to craft solutions. The redescribing doesn't change the situation, just the tone and meaning. Such redescribing helps the school counselor focus his or her energy on assisting the student employ abilities he or she already possesses with increasing flexibility and adaptability in the school setting.

Louie: Yeah, I'm always gettin' in trouble, 'cause I'm hyperactive.

Counselor: Hyperactive? Are you saying that you are never able to sit still or pay attention? I thought you told me you played catcher on the school's baseball team?

Louie: Yeah . . . so ?

Counselor: Well, I would think that when you are catching, you need to pay attention to the pitcher?

Louie: I'd get hit on the head if I wasn't paying attention. I love to play baseball. I made the all-star team this year as starting catcher! Plus, I set the school record for picking off guys trying to steal second base—I had eleven pickoffs.

Counselor: Wow . . . that took a lot of concentration . . . and a real "gun" for an arm!

Redescribing the situation without problem speak doesn't change or minimize the behavior but it does invite the student to see him or herself differently and the situation more hopefully. As suggested by this brief exchange, the solution-focused school counselor is less interested in why the student called out and got out of his seat (the "problem") and more eager to discover how this same student is able keep his attention on both a pitcher and a runner at first base. Discovering the skills this student uses to be successful in the sporting arena may provide the counselor and the student with a bounty of resources to craft a strategy to generalize towards success in the classroom.

Another illustration of this paradigm shift and movement away from problem speak can be seen in the following brief exchange between a school counselor and a senior high school student in jeopardy of not graduating due to a failing grade in a specific class.

George: I know . . . I know. I'm failing. Big deal!

Counselor: George (looking at transcript), I know you are failing social studies. What surprised me is that you are passing the other majors. Wow. How did you do that?

           (Redirecting from problem to success)

George: (Surprised and with less of a defensive tone) How do I do what?

Counselor: Well, I'm looking here and you have a C in math, a B in chemistry, and an A in English literature. I know these are not easy courses, so that's pretty impressive. Whatever you are doing in those classes, it is working! I just wonder how you do that. What do you do to get those grades? I think if we can figure that out, then maybe we could use that information somehow?

The counselor in the above illustration failed to respond to the initial and defensive problem speak offered by the student, "I know . . . I know. I'm failing. Big deal!" Focusing the discussion on the failing grade—the failures—and the student as "failing" would only elicit more defensiveness and perhaps hopelessness. The solution-focused counselor is interested in successes and goal attainment. The redirection that occurred in this session has positioned the counselor and student to investigate arenas where he is successful. Identifying what he does and how he does it—in those situations—provides the raw ingredients for crafting an approach to moving from a failing grade in social studies to a passing grade.

Creating a Uniquely Collaborative Relationship

Littrell (1998) stated, "Strategies and techniques are ineffectual if the facilitative conditions of warmth, genuineness, and empathy do not permeate the counseling process" (p. 8). As with any model of counseling, the quality and nature of the relationship between the student and the school counselor remains an important variable in the outcome of solution-focused counseling.

The therapeutic alliance is essential for the solution-focused counselor. But it is not just the creation of a warm, accepting, nonjudgmental relationship that is sufficient. For the school counselor employing a solution-focused orienting model, creation of a cooperative, collaborative relationship with the student is needed (Watts & Pietrzak, 2000).

In the initial phase of engagement with the student, "joining" and building a foundation for cooperative work is fostered through discussion with the student (Berg, 1994). The school counselor joins with students by employing fundamental helping skills, setting them at ease, conveying nonjudgmental interest, and avoiding the various forms of lecturing, advice giving, and nagging that students often have been subject to by the time they have reached the counselor's office. The message conveyed by the solution-focused school counselor is: (1) the student, and his or her goals take precedence; and (2) the competencies, experiences, and resources brought to the counseling by the student are valued and will be employed. The solution-focused counselor believes that the student is an expert about his or her own life (De Jong & Berg, 1998) and, as such, brings valuable expertise and insight to the process. With this, the alliance or working relationship created and nurtured in solution-focused counseling is one where the student is viewed as an essential "resource" to the progress and outcome of the counseling process.

Solution-oriented writers have noted that advice giving tends to put people on the defensive (Berg, 1994). Students who feel defensive are not usually amenable to entering into a cooperative relationship with the counselor. Furthermore, lecturing and its variations tend to focus on "the problem" and generally provide more of a sense of relief for the advice giver rather than the achievement of the intended purpose: changing the student's behavior.

In developing this cooperative relationship, the solution-focused therapists will be alert to avoid interventions or strategies that might disturb this cooperative nature of the relationship. If the activity of the counselor—be it a recommendation for intervention or the pursuit of a specific topic—makes the student uncomfortable, the counselor should reconsider his or her course of action. For example, consider a student who is struggling with a mathematics class. While the counselor may feel that consulting with the teacher may be a useful strategy, if the student feels uncomfortable with this intervention or simply passively accepts it, the solution-focused counselor would back off—at least at this point—to engage the student in the student's view of an alternative plan.

This does not mean that the counselor passively sits and takes complete direction from the student allowing him or her to discuss only topics of comfort and avoid areas which may be somewhat challenging. While respecting and joining the student as co-equals in the relationship, the school counselor, employing a solution-focused orienting framework, accepts the responsibility to guide the process of change. As such, a counselor—while affirming and allowing the student to share his or her story the way he or she chooses to do—would listen for constructive possibilities that can be used at a later time. Consider the following exchange and note how the counselor both respects the student's desire to give shape and direction to the exchange while at the same time invites the student to engage in discussion and reflection in another direction.

Thomas:	So, she's always picking on me. Everybody else in class screws around and never gets punished. I look the wrong way and she gives me detention!
Counselor:	So, you feel that Mrs. Alberts is always picking on you? Hmm . . . I wonder if there are times when she isn't?
Thomas:	No, she is always after me. She doesn't like me. Everybody else in class can talk and clown around but not me . . . I hate her.
Counselor:	Thomas, when Mrs. Alberts is giving you detention, what is it that you may be doing?
Thomas:	Nothing! She just doesn't like me. I want to get out of her class.
Counselor:	It sounds like the class hasn't been much fun for you? It also seems that you think it would work better if you could get out of that class. How would that work for you?
Thomas:	I don't know. Maybe another teacher wouldn't be so mean.
Counselor:	Do you have some teachers who, as you say, aren't so mean?
Thomas:	Yeah—a lot. Mrs. Pearson's class is great . . . I love it.
Counselor:	Oh, that's great! What do you do to help make her class one you love?

The counselor in this brief exchange wanted to have Thomas look at his own behavior in Mrs. Alberts's class and see how that was working. The student expressed some discomfort with this strategy and thus the counselor allowed the student as collaborator to give shape to the direction of the conversation. While allowing the student to continue to externalize the problem as one in which he was victim to Mrs. Alberts, the counselor attended and listened for an opportunity to once again invite Thomas to consider his own behavior, and the impact his choices may have on the experience within a classroom. Hopefully, having Thomas identify his actions and decisions in Mrs. Pearson's class may provide the raw materials for structuring a mini-experiment to try in Mrs. Alberts's class—an experiment that would truly be the outcome of a collaborative exchange.

This process of approaching the relationship as co-equals may be difficult for counselors who are acculturated to believe that adults always know best, and also hard for students who have been shaped to dismiss their perspectives in search of the adult expertise. The solution-focused counselor knows that engaging the student as expert reduces defensiveness and increases the sense of hope and excitement.

Meeting the Student at His or Her Model of the World

School counselors are usually pretty skilled at building rapport with their students. During initial engagement, rapport building may take the form of "small talk" which may even be on matters unrelated to the referral. But with a solution-focused orienting framework, the skills used and the goals desired extend beyond the development of rapport. The solution-focused school counselor attempts to truly meet the student at his or her model of the world.

In joining the student, the counselor may choose to employ the ideas, metaphors, and even the exact language of the student. It would not be unusual for the counselor, attempting to join with the student, to match the student's language. For instance, students may talk about a teacher or parent who is "bugging" or that somebody has a "tude." While not attempting to sound like a peer, or someone who is trying to be "cool" or "in," the solution-focused school counselor may reflect the words employed, even asking for clarification and elaboration. For example, the counselor, upon hearing a student refer to a teacher as having a "tude," might respond by stating, "A 'tude'? What would be a sign that the teacher's 'tude' was getting better?"

The school counselor employing a solution-focused orienting framework literally joins the student in his or her lived reality. In our previous example, the counselor working with Thomas isn't interested in debating the validity of his observations or in defending his teacher. Rather, the counselor wants to join Thomas in his "here and now" experience of the classroom as a place where he feels singled out for punishment. This process is not meant to affirm the objective reality, since for the solution-focused counselor, the focus is on the subjective construction of reality as it impacts one's experience. The counselor will attempt to more fully understand this "reality" of being singled out. Does it happen all the time? Does it happen only in this class or others? Are there exceptions? These questions are not meant as challenges to the student but rather invitations for clarification.

This process of joining the student at his or her model of the world is not only essential for the establishment of a trusting and understanding relationship, but also for the identification of goals that are meaningful to the student. Joining the student with his or her model of the world allows the counselor to accept the student's initial goals, even if these appear to be less important to the counselor.

The counselor with a solution-focused orienting framework values the importance of identifying what is important to the student, since it is the student who will serve as the primary source of resources needed to achieve these goals. This is not to suggest that counselors won't be alert to inviting a redefining or reframing of the student's reality as a means of facilitating additional goal achievement. For example, consider the counselor working with a student who, while failing, is expressing concerns about being rejected by his friends. The counselor may feel that the priority should be grades first, friends second, but the principle of joining the student in his world directs the counselor to embrace the student's goal as taking primacy—trusting that other goals will emerge. Perhaps in this situation, the counselor learns that the student is failing because he is not completing his homework. Further, it becomes clear that he is not completing his homework because he does not take his text or materials home. In discussing this with the student, the counselor finds out that the student feels he cannot "risk" taking books home, since he is sure his "boys" would get on his case and eventually kick him out of the group. While some may suggest that this student simply get a different group of friends or have the courage to stand up for what he values, the solution-focused counselor values the student's goal to be accepted as taking center stage. With the goal of maintaining his social inclusion, along with a goal of passing his classes, the student, in cooperation with the solution-focused counselor, begins to identify strategies that could be used to successfully achieve *both* goals. In this case, the solution may come in the form of providing multiple sets of textbooks, one set for school that could be left in the locker and one set for home where homework could be completed. Or, perhaps the student would like to use the study hall period to be "called down" to the counselor's office, where he could privately complete his work. In either case, the creativity of the solution reflects the resources of the student and addresses the goals—both grades and social acceptance—deemed important by the student.

This process of meeting the student in his or her world can be quite a challenge for the counselor, especially if the counselor enters the relationship believing that he or she knows best. It is true that we have different experience, perspectives, and skills—that is not the issue. The principle of "joining the student" means that rather than demanding that the student embrace our worldview, that we assist the student in the process of change by embracing his or her needs, goals, and resources.

The process of meeting the student in his or her world can be somewhat disconcerting and disarming to the student, especially when his or her previous experience has led to expectations that the adult will impose the "way things should be." When that imposition does not occur and the student is invited to give shape to the goals and strategies to be employed, a major source of resistance and defensiveness is removed and cooperation can emerge.

Focusing on the Present and the Future, and Not the Past

The solution-focused school counselor truly embraces the student where he or she is at this point in time. Embracing the value of the student "as is" at this moment, and helping the student articulate a desired future, sets the stage for developing the belief that choice and change are possible. With this focus on the present as the springboard to the desired future, the school counselor establishes the premise that where a student is today need not be where he or she is tomorrow. The message delivered is that the student's future is not fixed or predetermined by the past, but rather can truly be crafted from the present.

This emphasis on the present and future doesn't mean the solution-focused school counselor discounts or ignores the past. However, when there is a discussion of the past, the solution-focused counselor targets that discussion on the identification of times and circumstances when the student experienced some, or all, of the desired goal. Looking at both the past and the now and searching for experiences which parallel the desired future sets the stage for investigating how the desired events came about.

The solution-focused counselor views students as having the resources to solve their own problems (Berg & Miller, 1992). Value is given to the present and the past only in that they provide a context to identify the resources that can be used to achieve the desired future state. This was the case of the counselor working with Maria, a fourth-grade student who was referred to counseling for what the teacher described as "extreme shyness," and yet a review of her history suggested that under certain conditions she could be quite a "performer."

Counselor: Maria, thanks for sharing. It sounds like you almost feel sick to your stomach when you think that you may be called upon to go to the board.

Maria: Yes, I don't know why, but I really don't want to go to the board; it makes me so scared and sweaty. I feel like everybody is looking at me.

Counselor: So, is this how you feel anytime you have to do something in front of other people?

Maria: I'm not sure what you mean.

Counselor: Well, have you ever played music or danced or maybe played in a sporting event . . . something like that?

Maria: Well, I take violin lessons. Is that what you mean?

Counselor: That's neat—violin, huh? Does your teacher ever ask you to play a song for the teacher, or your parents?

Maria: Each year, we have a recital where we all perform and our parents and grandparents and friends can come.

Counselor: Wow! That sounds really neat. You mean that all the students who take lessons perform on stage in front of a real audience?

Maria: Yes, we do it right here at school. They have a pamphlet that has everyone listed along with the songs they will play. I play in a quartet but I also have a solo.

Counselor: I am so impressed. That is really neat. Maybe you could let me know when the next recital is and, if you wouldn't mind, I would love to come.

Maria: Sure. I would like you to come.

Counselor: You know, Maria, I was wondering. I know you said you get nervous when called to the front of the class, but here you are in front of all of these people, on stage . . . with a solo, and you are able to do it. How do you do that?

With this point of reference, the counselor will guide Maria through an investigation of how she is able to focus and relax enough to play her violin in a formal performance. These data will serve as the resource base from which the counselor and Maria can develop strategies that will help her generalize this confidence to her performance in the classroom.

Starting With the End in Mind

As suggested by the name "solution focused," a core principle guiding practice is to place emphasis on a preferred future, a goal, which would reflect the resolution of the current situation. This shift in emphasis from cause to goal is a clear shift in paradigm. For counselors employing a solution-focused model, discussion around issues of "curing," "fixing," and "pathology," or "problems" is replaced by the construction of hopeful goal realities.

The principle of "starting with the end in mind" directs the school counselor to assist the student in identifying a desirable end point. The solution-focused counselor will follow the students' desires and help them frame goals that meet their preferences, even when that end point identified may not be one that was the counselor's first choice.

This principle of focusing on end points—goals, rather than problems and pathology—is clearly in line with the role and function of the school counselor whose primary service is promoting student development and achievement. It is a principle that the school counselor employing a solution-focused orientation uses, even from the earliest moments of the encounter. Unlike counselors employing more traditional models, the solution-focused school counselor won't initiate contact with questions about the problem. Rather than inviting the student to, "Tell me about your problem" or, "How can I help you?" the solution-focused—end in mind—counselor asks, "What would you like to change?" or, "What would you hope to see happen as a result of coming to talk with me?" These questions immediately focus the student on what he or she wishes—the goals desired—rather than on what was and what is undesirable. Consider the following interaction between Mrs. "T" (a counselor with a "traditional" orientation) and Jerome, a middle school, sixth-grade student.

Mrs. T: Well, Jerome, maybe you can help me understand a little bit about what's going on in study hall and why you are always getting in trouble?

Jerome: I don't know.

Mrs. T: According to Mr. Farve, you are always talking and disrupting the people around you. Is there something going on that you can tell me about?

Jerome: No . . .

Mrs. T: Jerome, I really would like to help you but you have to tell me what's going on?

Jerome: I don't know . . . Mr. Farve is always on my case.

Contrast this interaction with the one that follows. In this second illustration, Mrs. "SF" (a counselor with a "solution-focused" orientation) targets goal identification as the primary concern, rather than pursuing a detailed description of the problem or identification of the possible cause.

Mrs. SF: Well Jerome, I see Mr. Farve is asking you to come and talk to me.

Jerome: Yeah.

Mrs. SF: If you and I are really successful today, what do you think would change that would make you feel that this was a good idea to come talk to me?

Jerome: I don't know.

Mrs. SF: Yeah, that may be hard to answer. But I wonder what could happen that may make Mr. Farve happy that he asked you to come see me?

Jerome: He'd probably be happy if I stopped clowning around in study hall and sat there quietly doing my work.

Mrs. SF: That's good. So, you think Mr. Farve would think this was a good idea if, as a result of coming here, you began to sit quietly in study hall and do your school work. That's good. But, how about you? What would you like to see happen because you came here?

Jerome: I guess that I won't be getting in trouble in study hall.

By targeting the identification of the end state or goal, rather than becoming absorbed in the analysis of the student or the student's problem, the counselor helps reduce the student's defensiveness and set the stage for expected change (Goldenberg & Goldenberg, 2000). Focusing on the positive, and what is possible, is a primary principle of the solution-focused approach.

Transforming the Student From a "Complainant" to a "Customer"

The solution-focused counselor wants the student to come to counseling with a clear goal and direction in mind, and an eagerness to engage in the process. However, that is not the typical context of many of our encounters.

Many of the students, like Jerome, come to the counselor's office at the request of another, perhaps a parent, teacher, or administrator. Sometimes when a student is sent to the counselor's office, he or she comes in protest, as if forced against his or her will. These students enter the counseling relationship often not really understanding why they are there, or when they do, not owning the value of the visit.

Students entering a counseling relationship at the request of another or without truly owning the value of the process arrive in counseling in what Berg and Miller (1992) have termed a "visitor" mode. A student in visitor mode is in counseling in body only, not in spirit. They arrive without intention of making any personal changes. The visitor typically does not believe that there are problems that need to be worked on, and the central goal is to end contact with the counselor as soon and as painlessly as possible.

A student entering as a visitor—not intending to stay or engage—may at best become a complainant. "Stuck" in the counselor's office, the student spends time complaining about the teacher, parents, or other students who, in the student's mind, are really the problem and the ones responsible for his or her difficulty. This was certainly the experience that Ms. "S" confronted when meeting with Bill.

Ms. S: Hi Bill. Thanks for coming down.

Bill: Sure. No problem.

Ms. S: Bill, according to Mrs. Morton, you were very disrespectful to her today in class.

Bill: Me! Yeah, right. She asked where my homework was and when I started to explain that I left it in my mom's car, she rolled her eyes and said loud enough for everyone to hear, "Oh, so the dog ate it!" These teachers treat you like you are an idiot. I know what sarcasm looks like. I have a right to be respected, too. So, I am the one who should be complaining.

Clearly, Ms. S has her work cut out for her. But the key is not to simply confront Bill, but to move him from being a complainant to becoming a "customer." As it now stands, Bill is only interested in enlisting Ms. S to serve as advocate and coconspirator against these teachers. The task for Ms. S, as a solution-focused counselor, is to transform Bill into an active, hopeful participant in the counseling process, a role that has been described as being a "customer" (Berg & Miller, 1992). According to Berg & Miller, a "customer" is a person who will actively participate in the counseling, appreciating the value of counseling and the resources students bring to the process.

One of the ways a counselor could assess if the student is coming as a "customer" is to identify the degree to which the student contributes to framing the goals and outcome of counseling. O'Connell (1998) suggested the ideal customer would present with a very clear idea of what is wanted to achieve and would come willing to invest effort into the changes needed to be made in order to achieve this outcome. A customer is the student who enters the counselor's office with the message, "I know where I am and where I want to be." The student, as customer, conveys that he or she recognizes the work it will take to move toward his or her goals, and once knowing that he or she has made progress, asks for support and assistance in continuing this hard work. Wow . . . if only! If only our students truly knew what they wanted and accepted the need to work to get it. Sometimes they do. However, when they don't, and present instead as "visitor" or "complainant," the primary task of the school counselor is to facilitate their development into the roles of "customers."

While specific strategies geared to moving our students into the role of customer will be discussed in the upcoming sections, suffice it to say that it is in joining our students in their world—embracing their goals and resources and keeping our focus on what can be, rather than picking at what was or was not—that we invite our students to become customers of counseling.

Understanding "If it Ain't Broke (in the Student's Mind), Don't Fix It"

An additional operational assumption held by the solution-focused school counselors is that students are not *always* experiencing failure. The school counselor operating from a solution-focused orienting framework values and employs the resources and strategies that have served the student well in the past, and brings these to bear on the current situation. This is a departure from the more traditional approaches that often engage the counselor in the development of complicated interventions and require a rewiring of the student in the attempt to "fix" what is broken. Since the reality is that what a student does actually works in many aspects and arenas of the student's life, a solution-focused school counselor attempts to identify these things that work, rather than fix something assumedly broken.

The solution-focused counselor approaches counseling believing that every student is successful. Focusing on even slight exceptions to problem experience, and finding times of goal achievement, will help the counselor and student identify possible solutions to the current situation, which become empowering for the student as they begin to recognize previously unnoticed successes that can be expanded and repeated (Berg & Miller, 1992).

Consider the student who is sent to the counselor's office because he or she is "unmotivated." That child is not unmotivated. That same child may be motivated to avoid schoolwork, or motivated to engage with peers, or motivated to engage in something else. The fact that the student is not engaged in school assignments is not evidence that the child is unmotivated. The school counselor with a solution focus is not concerned about fixing this lack of motivation; rather attention is turned to how to help this student employ his or her ability to motivate him- or herself in others areas of his or her life and then generalize that skill to the task of school assignment. The same would be true for the child who is sent to the office for "always getting in trouble." While a counselor with a traditional approach may wonder, "What's wrong with her?" the solution-focused counselor would suggest . . . maybe nothing. It may be that getting into trouble is, in some way, "working" for that child. The task for the solution-focused school counselor is to step into that child's world to understand how this process works for the child. It is in this understanding that the counselor may be able to introduce alternative strategies for achieving the goal, while reducing the costs.

The solution-focused counselor values the efficacy and attempts to identify the student's talents, abilities, style, and ways of successfully adapting. Once identified, these "successes" will be affirmed and the student will be invited to creatively consider ways to expand their use. As suggested by Berg and Miller (1992) useful mantras to be used by the solution-focused counselor could be:

"If it ain't broke, don't fix it."

"Once you know what worked, do more of it."

"If it doesn't work, don't do it again. Do something different."

This principle allows the counselor to identify strategies that require the least amount of resource drain, and thus are more attractive to a student for whom "change" is already costly.

Valuing Small Steps and Small Changes

As a constructivist, the solution-focused counselor values the power of creating and embracing positive expectations. Helping the student see "problems" as periodic interruptions to his or her healthy functioning, rather than as irrevocable impediments or character flaws, provides the context to inspire hope and belief in the possibility of change (Nunnally, 1993). This position is affirmed when change is expeditious both in terms of speed and resource allocations. Small changes show evidence of progress—evidence that affirms the expectations of success.

Ted: Well, I almost made it.

Counselor: Almost?

Ted: Yeah. Well, after our talk yesterday, I decided that I would stop smoking. And I was doing pretty good. All the guys were hanging out after school and doing a joint. But I just told them no thanks, and that I wasn't into it today.

Counselor: That's fantastic. How did you do that? I mean, how were you able to say no thanks?

Ted: Don't get too excited. Later that night, Jeff called and we went out and I got stoned.

Counselor: That must have been tough, and I bet a bit disappointing, since you had previously made up your mind to stop smoking. It sounds like it is something that is hard to stop . . . but we both know you took a good step in that direction. Not only did you commit to stopping, but you really were successful after school with the guys. So, I'm still impressed that you were able to say "no" earlier . . . and I bet if we figure out how you did that, then maybe you could do it again.

As is evident from the above brief exchange, and as will be elaborated upon within the sections to follow, the solution-focused school counselor is very affirming and quick to highlight student success, even when that success is but a small step in the desired direction. This affirmation not only reinforces the success and sets the expectations of success, but truly also provides the data from which to expand successful practice.

FINAL THOUGHTS

In the sections to follow, we will discuss specific strategies and techniques employed by solution-focused school counselors. However, it is important to once again highlight the fact that these strategies, these techniques, emerge from and are reflections of the underlying philosophy and principles discussed within this chapter.

In order to effectively process the data presented by students, and in turn craft these data into meaningful interventions, the school counselor needs to go beyond the simple menu-driven application of techniques. It is essential that the school counselor not only employs the lens of a solution-focused counselor, but also assimilates the worldview and conceptual framework outlined within this chapter. As we end this chapter, it may be helpful to review the following comparative table, Table 2.2, as it highlights the uniqueness of this approach. Reviewing the table may serve as a check and balance to your own conceptualization of counseling.

Table 2.2 Comparing Problem-Focused and Solution-Focused Models

Problem-Focused Models	Solution-Focused Models
Key assumptions: Patterns are stable over time. Pathology impairs choice, control, and personal development. Students are impaired and in need of remediation.	**Key assumptions:** Change is constant and inevitable. Possibilities for choice, control, and development are always open. Students are capable experts on own lives.
Role of helper: Expert on what's wrong and what to do to correct what's wrong. Prescriptive and directive. Hierarchical relationship. Certainty in perspectives.	**Role of helper:** Expert on helping access and apply student competence toward self-defined goals. Dialogic and co-constructive. Collaborative partnership. Curiosity in possibilities.
Diagnose psychopathology/ assess problems: Symptom patterns (frequency, severity, duration, impact, etc.). History and trauma (viewed as predictive of psychopathology). Hypothesis about causality. Symptom classification. Diagnosis. Prognosis.	**Assess solutions/evaluate resources:** Student's desired outcomes (goals). Social context and construction of student's meanings. Student's frame of reference. What works for each unique student. Exceptions to problems. Skills and capabilities. Coping resources.
Counselor's actions: Empathize, support, reframe, clarify, interpret, educate, advise, direct, assign, encourage catharsis. Determine what student needs. Design interventions to match problems.	**Counselor's actions:** Affirm, validate, normalize. Invite student self-direction. Encourage using what already works. Discuss student's possible next steps.
Data source for interventions: Professional theories and knowledge. Skills and resources of counselor as expert.	**Data source for interventions:** Strengths, abilities, creativity, ideas, and skills of both student and counselor in cooperation.

SOURCE: Adapted from Berg, 1992.

SUMMARY

More Than Just New Techniques:
A New Perspective and a Shift in Paradigm

- Nelson (1998) suggested that the first step in becoming a solution-focused counselor is to change our thinking.
- Solution-focused counselors adhere to a constructivist philosophy believing we do not have direct access to objective truth and reality, rather, we are dependent on our linguistically constructed versions of reality.
- The solution-focused school counselor uses problem-free language (George, Iveson, & Ratner, 1990) and shifts his or her focus away from problems, causes, and pathology to goals and successes.
- For the solution-focused school counselor, "problems" are not indications of something fundamentally wrong with the student; they simply are experiences that occur in the natural flow of human interaction.

Fundamental Principles Guiding Solution-Focused Practice

- The solution-focused counselor, as a constructivist, avoids "problem talk" and helps the students reframe their stories, their lived experiences, in positive ways so that they see themselves as more competent and their futures more hopeful.
- While the therapeutic alliance and core conditions are needed, the school counselor employing a solution-focused orienting model values the creation of a cooperative and collaborative relationship with the student.
- Joining the student in his or her worldview is considered essential to the solution-focused school counselor. The counselor with a solution-focused orienting framework values the importance of identifying what is important to the student, since it is the student who will serve as the primary source of resources needed to achieve these goals.
- The solution-focused counselor targets the "now" and the "future" as key to the counseling process and, while not denying or ignoring the importance of the past, finds value in the past only

(Continued)

(Continued)

to the degree that it provides illustrations of the student's successful coping and adapting skills.

- A core principle guiding practice is to place emphasis on a preferred future, a goal, which reflects the resolution of the current situation. Rather than engaging in elaborate diagnosis or problem identification and cause articulation, the solution focus turns attention to the identification of a desired future state.
- The solution-focused counselor attempts to engage students as "customers" in counseling, people who will actively participate in the counseling, appreciating the value of counseling and the resources they bring to the process.
- The solution-focused counselor believes that students have been and can be successful and simply need to reengage in those things that worked, rather than fix things assumedly broken. This is another departure from the more traditional approaches where counselors often engage in the development of complicated interventions requiring a rewiring of the student in their attempt to "fix" what is broken.
- Small changes show evidence of progress—evidence that affirms the expectations of success and thus is actively affirmed by the solution-focused school counselor.

Part II

Solution-Focused Discourse and the Strategies Employed

Similar to counselors using other orienting frameworks, school counselors operating from a solution-focused framework also employ specific techniques to help facilitate a student's movement toward a desired goal. Somewhat unique to a solution-focused approach, however, is that interventions are not something done *to* the student, but rather done *with* the student.

The strategies employed by a solution-focused counselor are not typical "interventions" in that they do not target the repair of a deficit, or the remediation of some pathology or sickness. This is a clear departure from the more classical models, which provide the counselor with a set of "interventions" which are to be employed—and often "applied" to the student as a means of correcting, modifying, or remedying the problematic situation.

The solution-focused counselor does not bring a bag of cures or interventions to the session. Rather, the solution-focused school counselor comes to the relationship attending to the student's story and prompting the student, through artful questioning and purposeful discourse, to identify desired goals, personal resources, and creative solutions.

As will become clear, the solution-focused school counselor is not merely chatting or holding a conversation. The discourse employed is a well-thought, dynamic, helping process. Part II presents a detailed discussion of three main themes that emerge in this process of solution-focused counseling. These themes are those involving discourse on change (Chapter 3), solutions (Chapter 4), and strategies (Chapter 5). However, prior to taking an in-depth look at these forms of discourse, a caveat is in order.

On first read, these "strategies" may appear rather simple, especially when compared to the elaborate and complex techniques presented by other counseling models. It is important that we do not let the apparent simplicity be misleading. These strategies are not simple tools to be applied in some formulaic approach. The process is neither rigid nor sequential. The solution-focused counselor engages in flexible movement between solution/problems, past/future, and goals/strategies in response to the individual student's needs (O'Connell, 1998).

Each strategy gains its value by way of the masterful timing and application at the hands of the effective school counselor. Just as a child may be able to make a sound with a simple slide whistle, in the hands of a musician this simple instrument can produce beautiful music. The same is true for the discourse and strategies employed in solution-focused counseling. When employed by a reflective school counselor, the simplicity of the strategy elicits the wonder of a student's story and the efficiency of creative solutions facilitating goal achievement.

Highlighting the Possibility and Process of Change   **3**

A n initial form of discourse found within solution-focused counseling emphasizes the process and possibility of *change* (O'Connell, 1998). The solution-focused school counselor engages in discussion with the student highlighting the expectation that not only is change possible, but that it is already taking place and will be facilitated by the counseling process.

Unlike a counselor who sees the student's presence in his or her office as a place to begin identifying problems and then eventually employing strategies to facilitate change, the solution-focused school counselor embraces the fact that the very presence of the student in the counselor's office is evidence that change has already taken place. Even when the student is mandated to go to counseling, the process of embracing that mandate and following through, thus resulting in the student's presence in the office, announces some change in the client's thinking, motivation, and actions. Which of these changes are facilitating movement toward desired goals, how they were initiated, and how they can be maintained are all targets for discussion within the early stages of the solution-focused relationship.

Counselor: Aretha, thanks for coming.

Aretha: I had to—Mr. Olsen sent me.

Counselor: Well, I know Mr. Olsen asked you to see me, but you heard him, and decided to come down, and I think that is a good start. In fact, I am really curious of how you did that?

Aretha: Did what?

Counselor: Well, I am sure you have had other people tell you to do things and you decided, "No thanks, don't want to!" But here, you decided to do it. How did you decide that?

Aretha: I don't know . . . I guess I didn't want him on my case.

Counselor: Oh, so you saw coming here as a way of getting Mr. Olsen to be more positive toward you. That's neat. Would that be a goal we work on . . . getting a better relationship with Mr. O?

The brief exchange occurring within the initial moments of this counselor's interaction with a student highlights the uniqueness of the counselor's focused discourse. While reflecting the client's "protest" in being sent, the counselor artfully redirected the discussion to affirm the student's decision to come as a first step toward change and goal achievement.

The responsibility for the direction of this discourse rests with the school counselor. The solution-focused counselor has an agenda for the nature and direction of the counseling session. This agenda is evident in the control the solution-focused counselor takes right from the "get-go." Rather than passively awaiting a student's request or disclosure, the solution-focused counselor will structure the encounter with questions focusing attention on a desired goal. For example, following an initial greeting, a counselor may invite the student to identify a goal for this initial session by asking, "What could happen in working together today that would demonstrate that it was a good idea for you to come to counseling?" This same type of active control and direction giving occurs in follow-up sessions as the solution-focused school counselor greets the student with questions such as, "What's better?" (Berg, 1992) or, "What's changed since our last session?" The purpose of these questions is to craft the session in a positive direction, highlighting the expectation that positive change can and has occurred.

While the hope for this discourse is to set the structure and process in place to have change occur, the solution-focused counselor joins with the student and values the reality that at any one time the student may be unable to fully respond in such *change discourse*. As noted previously, this is not a formula for linear sequenced steps. The solution-focused counselor works in cooperation with the student and allows the student to give direction even when that direction engages discussion of the past, or the problem, or the externalization of the responsibility for the current situation. These diversions from change discourse are respected and allowed, since they are evidence that the student is not able or ready to engage in discussion of change.

In situations such as these, the solution-focused counselor will turn his or her attention to strengthening the working relationship and joining the student in his or her world in hopes of engaging the student as a "customer" in the counseling.

Counselor: Hi Loren. Thanks for coming.

Loren: Yeah, right.

Counselor: Loren, I'm glad you are here, and I'm wondering what might happen today as a result of us talking that would make you happy that you came?

Loren: I don't need to come. It's Ms. Pettaway's problem.

Counselor: Okay, so Ms. Pettaway is upset—but since you are here, I guess I was wondering what it is that you would like to have happen as a result of coming?

Loren: I'm here 'cause I have to be here, no offense. Why don't you go ask her?

Counselor: Actually, maybe we could talk about that. Talking to her may be good idea, and something for us to consider. So, tell me what is it that we may find out by talking to her?

While the counselor in this case attempted to redirect the student to begin to identify and articulate a preferred future—a goal for this session—it is clear that at this point in time Loren was not able or willing to embrace that orientation. The counselor, reflecting on the tone of this exchange, made the decision to redirect attention to strengthening the supportive nature of the relationship and joining Loren in her world, rather than to continue attempts at change discourse.

Loren: Probably that I'm screwing up or something, but she's got something up her butt. She's always on me.

Counselor: Always on you?

Loren: Yeah, her class is completely out of control, everybody is screwin' around and yet if I look the wrong way, she's all over me.

Counselor: So, it seems that she treats you differently than the other people in class?

Loren: Yeah, like she has it out for me. I don't know (sounding frustrated).

Counselor: You sound really frustrated. It seems you are acting like the other students and yet Ms. P corrects you in class?

Loren: I hate it (starting to tear).

Counselor: Loren, I can see you are upset and frustrated, and I'm wondering, is it like this in all of your classes?

Loren: No. I like my classes. I have Mr. Elison for English and it's great. I hate to hear the bell ending class knowing that Ms. P. is waiting for me.

Counselor: That's really interesting. You have Mr. Elison's class and that's something you really like. It almost sounds like that's the type of class experience you wish you had in Ms. P's class?

Loren: Yeah, but that isn't going to happen . . .

While encouraging Loren to direct the telling of her story, even when that directs the discussion toward problems, the counselor will continue to periodically test the water as to the ability to engage the student in change discourse. As evident by the above, Loren's introduction of Mr. Elison's class as a preferred scenario will allow the counselor to begin discussion about the unique characteristics of this experience and the specific ways Loren engages within that class. This discussion sets the stage for envisioning a different—changed—experience with Ms. P.

As a solution-focused counselor employs change discourse he or she will engage the student in problem deconstruction, competence talk, and exception talk.

PROBLEM DECONSTRUCTION

Students often present as being overwhelmed, "believing" their problem is monumental and unsolvable and that they (and everyone else) are helpless in making things better. Their experience of being helpless, with a life that is hopeless, is real. It is the constructed, subjective reality for these students that can result in their simply desiring to surrender, to throw their hands up, and throw in the towel.

The construction of this felt reality is often the result of the student being unable to gain clarity and focus on the specific situations or issues of concern. Much of this lived experience is a function of the vague, overly general and abstract words the student uses to construct and disclose their problem. When this is the case, the solution-focused school counselor will attempt to help the student deconstruct the problem, making it concrete and manageable, using *problem deconstruction*.

Counselor: Mai, please sit down (handing her a tissue). What's wrong? Why are you crying?

Mai: They hate me (crying).

Counselor: They?

Mai: Everybody.

Counselor: Everybody? Mai, maybe you could tell me what happened?

Mai: Liz and Maria were making fun of me at lunch. They called me a "poser" and a loser.

Counselor: So, the everybody you are talking about are Liz and Maria?

Mai: Nobody likes me (crying again).

Counselor: Mai, it sounds like Liz and Maria's comments really upset you, but when you say you have no friends, and nobody likes you . . . I'm confused. Are you saying it was everyone at lunch calling you a "poser" and a loser?

Mai: No. Rebecca and LuAnn were there and they were nice. They told Liz and Maria to stop picking on me.

Counselor: Oh, okay . . . so Rebecca and LuAnn were acting like they liked you and were trying to help you?

Mai: Yeah, they're nice.

Counselor: I think I understand. So, for some reason, Liz and Maria were teasing you. It wasn't that everyone was teasing you. In fact, it seems that Rebecca and LuAnn were being friendly?

Mai: Yeah (calming).

Counselor: I'm wondering, are Liz and Maria always teasing you, or are there times when you get along as friends?

In reviewing the above exchange, it is clear that Mai's initial world-view was one in which no one liked her. If that were true, it certainly would be overwhelming. As evident by the discourse that followed, that constructed worldview was not supported by the actual events of her life. The counselor's redefinition of the scope of this issue was a valuable step toward achieving a calmer, more hope-filled construction of Mai's world.

Similarly, consider the student who comes to counseling sharing the experience that he or she is "always in trouble." If we take the self-description as valid reflections of reality, then the problem we are presented is pretty monumental. How would we, or anyone, help someone who is *always* in trouble? Does that mean at this very moment the student is problematic, causing trouble in the counselor's office? Was he or she a problem in the hall on the way to the office? How about at home in his or her bedroom? If, in fact, the answer to all of these questions was "yes," then the scope of the problem along with nature of the "interventions" required would be significantly different than if the definition of *always* is narrowed to specific times and/or circumstances.

The purpose of the counselor's questions, which are somewhat challenging to the accuracy of the depth and breadth of the problem as presented by the student, is not to make light of the student's concern, or discount the felt experience. Rather, the goal of these challenging questions is to help highlight the need for the counselor and student to deconstruct this "massive" problem that is weighing the student down. The goal is to deconstruct the problem so that opportunities can be identified, and manageable obstructions can be defined, and then steps to their removal can start to emerge.

One student who initially felt her problem was so monumental that it was unsolvable presented her counselor with a very creative, artistic presentation of her "deconstructed" issue. This senior drew a picture depicting a huge elephant standing between her and her goal and gave this to her counselor as a "thank you." On first blush, it appeared to be an unusual "thank you" to the counselor who helped her navigate a significant issue in her life. However, as one looked more closely at the picture, what first appeared like a huge, wrinkled pachyderm, was in fact hundreds of tiny grey mice, arranged in a configuration resembling an elephant. The message was clear. What appears huge and immovable may more accurately be a series of smaller, easily removed obstacles to our goal achievement.

The school counselor focusing on problem-deconstruction discourse is alert to the nature of the problem as constructed by the student. Rather than simply embracing the student's definitions of the problem or self-descriptions as depressed or having low self-esteem, the solution-focused school counselor will invite the student to employ concrete, descriptive language in depicting how things are in day-to-day functioning. If we return to the illustration of the counselor working with Mai, it is clear that the counselor is helping the student move from a vague presentation of her social experience (i.e., no one likes me), to a more specific, concrete description of her lived experience. In this case, what begins to emerge is that rather than the "elephant" of having no friends, what really is happening is that two individuals appear to be teasing her. But the question remains, what is the actual frequency of this type of experience?

Counselor:	I think I understand. So, for some reason Liz and Maria were teasing you. It wasn't that everyone was teasing you. In fact, it seems that Rebecca and LuAnn were being friendly?
Mai:	Yeah (calming).
Counselor:	I'm wondering, are Liz and Maria always teasing you, or are there times when you get along as friends?
Mai:	We used to be really good friends.
Counselor:	Used to be?
Mai:	We are on the cheer squad and newspaper and we hang out.
Counselor:	Mai, you say you *are* on the cheer squad and newspaper and hang out . . . are you saying you still do that . . . you get along in those situations?
Mai:	Yeah . . . but why were they all over me today?
Counselor:	That's a good question. But before we begin to think about that, let me make sure I understand what we are working on. I know it felt like no one, or at least Liz and Maria, never liked you. But when we really look at it, what's upsetting is that these friends were for some reason teasing you at lunch today. Is that it?

A school counselor attempting to assist the student in deconstructing the problem, as depicted in the above exchange, focuses the discussion on concrete descriptions. This focus on specifics helps the student recognize that the problem is not as all encompassing as originally constructed, and that change is possible.

COMPETENCE TALK

A second process employed in change discourse is *competence talk*. The use of competence talk helps to reframe the discourse from a problem focus to one supporting the possibility of positive change.

Sadly, all too often, students coming for "help" come to counseling engulfed in "problems" and view their life from a deficit perspective. These students enter the counselor's office, head and spirit down, presenting as failing and a failure, in trouble and thus bad or unhappy and without hope.

Presenting oneself in a problem state leads to a focus and perhaps a discussion on the personal limitations and failures that have resulted in the creation of the current situation. Counselors employing "problem speak" ask questions that focus the student on the nature of the problem, the causes of the problem, and the role of the student in the creation and maintenance of the problematic situation. These sessions take form in questions such as:

"Okay, what did you do?"

"Why do you get yourself in these situations?"

"How long have you been feeling this way/doing this/acting this way?"

Even when the questions are sensitively posed, they remain invitations to engage in reconstructions of the student's problem experience and the articulation of those deficits that need "fixing."

In contrast, the solution-focused school counselor engages in "competence talk" in order to refocus the discourse on the real possibility of change. The identification of ways and means the student has coped in the past in this type of situation or in other arenas becomes an important target for the session. If we pick up the counselor discourse with Mai, we will see this focus on competence talk.

Counselor:	That's a good question. But before we begin to think about that, let me make sure I understand what we are working on. I know it felt like no one, or at least Liz and Maria, never liked you. But when we really look at it, what's upsetting is that these friends were for some reason teasing you at lunch today. Is that it?
Mai:	Yeah, I guess. But why do they do that?
Counselor:	I'm wondering, Mai. We know they do not do it all the time, but I bet today was not the only time they or somebody else has teased you?
Mai:	My older brother, Naijian . . . he's always . . . teasing me.
Counselor:	Older brothers can be pests sometimes. What do you do when he teases you?
Mai:	Sometimes I walk away, or tease him back, or tell my mom.
Counselor:	Wow, that's neat. So, when your brother teases you, you have all these ways of doing something, other than getting upset. I mean, sometimes you just walk away. Or sometimes you tease him back. And, if I understand correctly, there are times when you tell your mom and she helps.

Mai: Sometimes I tell my mom to get him in trouble (smiling).

Counselor: Okay (smiling), but those other things like walking away or teasing him back, that's cool. You really have some neat ways of dealing with teasing.

This exchange between the counselor and Mai, while not directly addressing positive ways to respond to Liz and Maria, is engaging the student in competence talk. With such "competence talk" the student's personal strengths and repertoire of behavior can be both affirmed and employed to solve the current situation (de Shazer, 1988).

In addition to the use of competence talk as a way of identifying student resources, the school counselor employing a solution-focused approach will engage the student in the process of *exception talk*.

EXCEPTION TALK

An extension of the competence talk, and an additional strategy to redirect hopeless expectations and problem speak to hopefulness and solution talk, is to engage the student in the investigation of exceptions to the current situation. As evidenced by the brief exchange between Mai and her counselor, Mai is not always teased, so in a sense there are times when "nonteasing" is an exception to this encounter. Further, we know that there are exceptions to Mai's crying in response to teasing, since she listed numerous alternative ways she responds to her brother's teasing. But how about times when teased by Liz and Maria? Is there ever a time when Mai does not break down in tears, or if upset, is less so than she presented on this occasion? These times would represent exceptions to her current "upset response" that may provide insight into the identification of her resources that are essential to resolving the current situation and fostering the achievement of a preferred future.

In engaging in exception talk, the solution-focused school counselor simply and directly invites the student to find those occasions or conditions in which the current "problem" either was not happening or was handled in a better way. Thus, for Mai, the counselor may want to seek an illustration in which Liz and Maria were really teasing her, but for some reason Mai employed one of those strategies she uses with her brother.

Counselor: Okay (smiling), but those other things like walking away or teasing back, that's cool. You really have some neat ways of dealing with teasing. I'm wondering, has there ever been a time when Liz and Maria were teasing you, and you used one of these strategies? You know, teased them back? Or maybe a time when you just ignored them, and walked away?

Mai: Hmm. You mean, like they were teasing me one time because I had a Hannah Montana T-shirt on and they we're saying, "Oh, look at Ms. Cool, the rock star." I just laughed and said, "I'd rather be a rock star than a rock" (smiling). I didn't know what that meant, but they laughed.

Counselor: Fantastic! That's what I was looking for—an exception to you getting upset about their teasing. Wow, that was great.

Identifying and owning the reality that exception did exist invites the student to reconstruct his or her absolute sense of the overwhelming and ever present problem, and thus open space for authoring a new, hopeful view of the future. This search for exception not only facilitates the student's deconstructing of the problem as immutable, but also begins to identify transferable solutions (Berg, 1992). This was illustrated in an exchange between Jerrone and his school counselor.

Counselor: I am really proud of you for wanting to stop smoking pot. I guess I could tell you all the reasons why, but what's really important is that stopping is something you really want to do.

Jerrone: Yeah, I really do, but I don't know if I can. All the guys I hang with smoke.

Counselor: All the guys?

Jerrone: Well, at least all the guys I hang with. And when we are hanging out and they are passing a joint, it's really hard to say no . . .

Counselor: I imagine it is hard. Has there ever been a time when you did say no . . . or at least did not smoke as much as you normally would?

Jerrone: Last Friday.

Counselor: Last Friday? Could you tell me what was happening?

Jerrone: We were all hanging after school . . . you know, the Friday "let's party" thing. Well, anyway, everyone starts to smoke and we had a couple of beers. But I didn't drink or smoke. I hung out for an hour and then went home.

Counselor: Wow! You hung out—without smoking or drinking. How did you do that?

Jerrone:	I just told them I wasn't going to party.
Counselor:	Super. But, how did you decide to do that?
Jerrone:	Oh, sorry. You know, I start for the football team? And we had the game Friday night against M. L. King High School. I just wanted to be sharp. Coach said college recruiters were going to be at the game.
Counselor:	Okay. So, being sharp and at your best for the game and the recruiters helped you to see that smoking and drinking would have interfered with that goal. Wow, that's great.

It appears that while it may be difficult for Jerrone to resist the subtle social pressure of smoking and drinking while hanging out with his friends, it is clear that when he feels that those activities will interfere with his achievement of desired goals, he is able abstain. The counselor in this situation will not only want to highlight and affirm this resource but then, along with Jerrone, craft strategies that will help him employ his future goals as a draw to pull him away from this type of partying behavior.

Now that the process of deconstructing the problem and reframing in terms of goal articulation has begun, and the counselor has helped increase the student's awareness of his or her competency and experiences of success, the stage is set for discourse on solution, a process discussed in the next chapter (Chapter 4).

SUMMARY

Change Discourse

- An initial form of discourse found within solution-focused counseling emphasizes the process and possibility of change (O'Connell, 1998).
- Unlike a counselor who sees the student's presence in his or her office as a place to begin identifying problems and then eventually employ strategies to facilitate change, the solution-focused school counselor embraces the fact that the very presence of the student in the counselor's office is evidence that change has already taken place.
- The solution-focused school counselor will structure the encounter with a questions focusing attention on a desired goal.

(Continued)

(Continued)

Problem Deconstruction

- Students often present as being overwhelmed, "believing" their problems are monumental and unsolvable and that they (and everyone else) are helpless in making things better. When this is the case, the solution-focused school counselor will attempt to help the student deconstruct the problem, making it concrete and manageable.
- The counselor will employ strategic questioning to challenge the student's perception of the depth and breadth of the problem in order to help the student to deconstruct this "massive" problem that is weighing them down.
- The goal is to deconstruct the problem so that opportunities can be identified, manageable obstructions can be defined, and steps to their removal can start to emerge.

Competence Talk

- The use of competence talk helps to reframe the discourse from a problem focus to one supporting the possibility of positive change.
- The identification of ways and means the student has coped in the past in this type of situation, or in other arenas, becomes an important target for the session.
- With such "competence talk," the student's personal strengths and repertoire of behavior can be both affirmed and employed to solve the current situation.

Exception Talk

- The solution-focused school counselor employing "exception talk" directly invites the student to find those occasions or conditions in which the current "problem" either was not happening or was handled in a better way.
- Identifying and owning the reality that exception did exist invites the student to reconstruct his or her absolute sense of the overwhelming and ever-present problem, and thus open space for authoring a new, hopeful view of the future.

Solution Identification and Implementation

4

The presentation of *solution discourse*, that is, the identification and implementation of solutions as a natural, sequential outgrowth of the previously discussed *change discourse* (Chapter 3), may be somewhat misleading. While separating these two points of focus for the school counselor employing a solution-focused model is a useful convention for textbooks, in practice, these two forms of discourse can occur simultaneously or a counselor may find drifting from one form of discourse to another, as the student permits, is also effective.

The processes grouped under the rubric of solution discourse all serve as intermediate interventions that help the student connect his or her current change processes with strategies that will be employed to obtain his or her goals (O'Connell, 1998). The specific strategies employed during this process of solution discourse include formation of collaboration relationship, setting and scaling goals, and assisting the student to reframe his or her current situation. Each of these strategies is described in detail in this chapter and illustrations of their application are presented.

COLLABORATIVE RELATIONSHIP

As noted previously, the solution-focused school counselor values the cooperative relationship of working with a student who engages in counseling as a "customer." This valuing of the student as an essential resource to the process of solution development and implementation cannot be understated. For the solution-focused school counselor, it is not merely the creation of a helper-helpee relationship, nor simple cooperation, that are sought. Rather, the solution-focused counselor attempts to move the relationship to one characterized as both mutual and co-equal and as such, truly collaborative.

The solution-focused school counselor employs all the core elements found in all effective counseling. In addition to the core conditions of warmth, genuineness, and unconditional positive regard, the solution-focused school counselor employs encouragement, provides compliments, and offers affirmations as the student's goals are identified and embraced. This last point needs to be highlighted because it truly is a unique characteristic of the solution-focused school counselor.

The solution-focused school counselor is committed to respecting and supporting what it is that the student wants to achieve. While the counselor may have ideas about what would be healthy and profitable for the student to achieve, the counselor values the principle of joining the client in his or her world and, as such, will embrace the student's goals as an essential, first step to counseling process.

In this collaborative relationship, the counselor brings his or her skills of questioning, summarizing, and reframing to the discourse in order to help the student identify goals that are useful and achievable. Thus, when a student presents the counselor with a goal such as "quitting school," the counselor accepts in principle that this goal must appear important to the student and thus must be embraced as a starting point. But, the counselor presented with such a goal may question the student in order to clarify if this was indeed the goal, or perhaps it was a perceived strategy to achieving a goal. Consider the following exchange.

Mr. P: Tory, glad to see you. What are we doing today?

Tory: I think I've had it. I'm really bored and failing things, since I'm not doing any work in class, and I just think this is a huge waste of time. So, I came down to ask you, what do I need to do to quit?

Mr. P: Tory, it sounds like you have given a lot of thought to this. That's good. You certainly don't want to rush into something this important. But, could you help me understand how quitting school, midway through your senior year, works for you?

Tory: Works for me?

Mr. P: Well, I mean, what do you do when you quit?

Tory: I'm not sure. I guess I would get a job. Anything would be better than coming day in and day out and being bored out of my mind.

Mr. P: So, it really sounds like your goal is be stimulated, to find enjoyment in your day, rather than being bored?

Tory: Yeah . . . you can't imagine how bad it is.

Mr. P: Well, I can imagine some things, but you are the one experiencing it. And if the issue or the goal is to somehow bring more stimulation, joy, and happiness to your day, maybe quitting school is one way, but I'm not really sure how that works.

Tory: I don't know . . . anything would be better than this.

Mr. P: Tory, I wonder what happens to our thinking if, rather than treating quitting school as an end point, you know a goal, that instead we look at it as one strategy which may, or may not, lead to your real goal—to be stimulated and happy during the day?

Tory: Why?

Mr. P: Well, if we leave it on the table as a possible strategy, then maybe we could identify other strategies that lead to feeling stimulated and happy throughout the day—and then we could see which strategy is the best?

The counselor in this scenario is not dismissing the student's goal as silly or undoable and is not engaged in a debate to argue against the student's presented goal. The counselor embraces the goal, the reality, as initially presented by the student and joins him in a collaborative discussion of the "what" and "what to be gained" by achieving this goal. Joining the student in this collaborative sharing allows the counselor to share the student's perspective.

The counselor understands that sometimes what a person identifies as a goal is really a strategy to the achievement of another, yet to be identified, goal. So, working in collaboration with the client, this counselor was able to help the student clarify his real goals, that is, to be stimulated, happy, and excited throughout his day. These appear both reasonable and achievable and provide a focal point for identifying multiple strategies for goal achievement. But, before attention shifts to the implementation of strategies for goal attainment, additional clarity is required.

THE MIRACLE QUESTION

A unique strategy that has come to typify the way a solution-focused counselor conducts an interview and frame each session is the use of the "miracle question." As defined by Berg & Miller (1992), the miracle question is a "[. . .] specially designed interview process . . . [which] orients the client away from the past and the problem and toward the future and a solution" (p. 13). It truly is a strategy and concept that is central to a solution-focused approach.

While the term "miracle" may lead one to conclude that the question is designed to encourage the student to place their faith in the occurrence of magic or miracles, this is not the case. The miracle question is simply a future-oriented question that invites the student to envision a future time when he or she and his or her world were exactly as they wished it to be. This future-oriented question is useful with goal setting since it shifts the focus from problems and their genesis to the unlimited range of possibilities when envisioning a preferred future.

The use of a miracle focus helps students access their creative capacities that are most adaptive when not constricted by the realities of life. The miracle question invites the student to think about change in ways that do not trigger thoughts that nullify the hope and belief in the possibility of achieving that change. The process invites the student to think out of the box. Students are asked to share their visions of preferred futures without concern for practical constraints or reality of current circumstances. The hope is to create the big picture of the changes the students would like to see.

While there is no strict formula for constructing the miracle question—the essence is conveyed in the following:

> Suppose that while you are sleeping tonight and the entire house is quiet, a miracle happens. The miracle is that the problem that brought you here is solved. However, because you are sleeping, you don't know that the miracle has happened. So when you wake up tomorrow morning, what will be different that will tell you that a miracle has happened and the problem that brought you here is solved? (de Shazer, 1985, p. 5)

If we look more closely at the question, a number of characteristics emerge. First, there is a soft reference to the fact that a problem or concern may be the basis for the student engaging in counseling, but the emphasis is immediately refocused on the preferred condition. The focus of this question is somewhat vague and open so as to allow the student the freedom to respond in any way that would be important to him or her. A student may respond with an emphasis on a changed self (e.g., I would control my temper; I would be able to wash my hands once and stop) or a changed context (e.g., my parents would be getting along; I would have friends at school). As noted, in joining in a collaborative relationship with the student, the counselor wants to understand and embrace the student's goal as an essential starting point to the counseling process.

The question doesn't invite conversation on how this is to be done or the resources and challenges one needs to address on the way to being successful. The purpose here is to begin the process of identifying goals so that the counselor and student can turn attention away from old, unsuccessful, past behaviors toward a future where the problem no longer exists.

With the emphasis on goals and solutions, the solution-focused counselor employs this strategy early in initial interactions and returns to it in subsequent sessions when the student begins to return to a problem-focused orientation. The counselor, after setting the student at ease, will listen for an appropriate moment to insert the question, as demonstrated by the following exchange.

Student: I really promised myself that today would be different, that I was going to come in here and not flip out, but here I am, did it again!

Counselor: So, you really made up your mind that this morning would be different. That's really good.

Student: Yeah . . . but I blew it . . . it's frustrating.

Counselor: It certainly makes sense that you may be frustrated, since it didn't work out the way you wanted. I'm wondering . . . just suppose, tonight when you go to bed and drift off to sleep that a miracle happens during the night, okay? Just imagine that this miracle is the type that would resolve the problem that brought you here.

Student: Hmm.

Counselor: But . . . remember, it's a miracle and you are asleep, so don't know it's happening.

Student: Okay.

Counselor: When you wake up tomorrow there will be signs, some evidence that the miracle has happened. What will you notice, what will give you the clues that maybe a miracle has happened?

The miracle question sets the stage for students to begin to identify the changes in self, others, and the world that they would prefer to that which they currently experience. It is important for the counselor to listen to the student as he or she identifies the clues that indicate a miracle has happened. The counselor, using the skills of reflection and clarification, will help increase the student's awareness of the goal that he or she is seeking.

Counselor: When you wake up tomorrow there will be signs, some evidence that the miracle has happened. What will you notice, what will give you the clues that maybe a miracle has happened?

Student: I guess I wouldn't be so grumpy. I would feel more relaxed and I would come downstairs happy . . . you know whistling or something like that.

Counselor: So, the first thing you would notice that told you a miracle happened is that you would feel and act more relaxed, happier?

Student: Yeah, and I would have all my stuff organized, and all of my work completed.

Counselor: That's super. So, in this miracle you would have your work completed, you would organize it and you would be ready to go to school in a relaxed and happy mood.

Student: Yeah . . . quite a miracle, huh (smiling)?

The student in our illustration has certainly begun to articulate goals, such as completing his work, organizing materials prior to going to school, or even relaxing—goals that are certainly achievable and will now provide the focal point for the counseling. Sometimes a student responds to the miracle question by stating that he or she would feel a certain way. While these are important, the solution-focused counselor will try to help the student identify what he or she would be doing differently that led to those feelings. The goal is to elicit statements that "include some action, some behavior, some new framing, or something clients will say to themselves or others" (Walter & Peller, 1992, p. 78). Thus, it is not simply asking the miracle question, but guiding the student in their development of that preferred future so that the material gathered can be used to concretize the goals and unearth strategies which may help in the process of goal achievement. Consider the assistance provided by the following counselor as he listened to his student, Donna, respond to the miracle question.

Counselor: Let's presume that when you go to sleep tonight a miracle has occurred. It is a miracle that will result in a major change for you. When you wake, you realize this miracle has transformed you. What would be the first thing that you would notice?

Donna: Probably that I didn't crawl back under the covers, stoned from the night before. Yeah . . . I'd actually get out of bed on time.

Counselor: Okay, so you'd notice you were on time and out of bed. Okay, and what else would you notice?

Donna: I hope that I, hmm, I wouldn't have a headache or that weird floating feeling? I'd be like really clearheaded.

Counselor: Okay, so you would notice that you could focus and your thinking was real clear and sharp? Okay, what else?

Donna: Oh, I would have great breath and a better taste in my mouth.

Counselor: Wow! So you'd have this great breath and good taste in your mouth and you would be jumping out of bed, real focused and clear in your thinking. That's super . . . anything else? Like maybe what would other people notice?

Donna: Yeah. Hmm . . . my mom would be shocked I was up and at breakfast and actually talking to her. She would be really happy and we would have a great talk over breakfast.

Counselor: That sounds nice. You'd be clearheaded and focused and sharing with mom while eating breakfast. That really sounds like a good start to your day.

Donna: She would probably be surprised how focused I was . . . and, like, motivated to get to school (laughing). She'd probably wonder who I was and what I did with her daughter!

Counselor: I guess that would be something really different for your mom, maybe like her daughter was back?

Donna: Yeah.

What is evident from Donna's descriptions is that she does "prefer" a future in which she is focused, clearheaded, motivated, communicative, and interacting positively with others. The use of the miracle question allowed her the freedom to get in touch with that desire and the freedom to articulate it. The skillful interaction with this counselor helped her develop her miracle state so that it is multidimensional, including cognition, social interactions, and physiology (remember the breath?)—but also in that it begins to give shape to the "what she needs to do" or solutions that will lead to this miracle. The ability to get out of bed and get moving in her day, clearheaded and focused, are responses to having gone to bed at a reasonable hour without the use of any drugs. Similarly, her pleasant attitude and interactional style served as stimulus for equally pleasant exchanges with her mom and perhaps others, like her teacher.

Thus goals and solutions are starting to be identified as a result of the miracle question.

Now, it's not unusual for a student, when presented with the miracle question, to give a somewhat unrealistic response. The solution-focused counselor knows how to reframe the question and employ reflections to help the student clarify his or her response in a way that would productively lead to the identification of achievable goals. For example, if the student responded, "I would inherit a billion dollars," the counselor can begin to drill down to workable goals by asking, "What would a billion dollars do for you?" or "How would having a billion dollars help solve this problem?" If the student responds, "People won't pick on me" or "I wouldn't have to worry about paying for college" or even "I could start to enjoy my life," the counselor has an opening to pursue these statements as goals that need additional clarification. The counselor's use of his or her skills of reflection, clarification, and summarization are essential in moving the student toward increased clarity and specification of the behaviors or decisions that he or she will be exhibiting in this new, preferred future.

SETTING EFFECTIVE GOALS

The miracle question sets the stage for goal articulation. For solution-focused school counselors, goals are expressed as beginnings rather than endings. The use of goals helps the counselor and student to get to work and be on track immediately (Walter & Peller, 1992, p. 55). The progress toward goals is both affirming and self-correcting. Goal talk helps the counselor assist the client to identify small signs of change or small steps to be taken to facilitate this change. This is the embodiment of the principle of starting with an end in mind.

Solution-focused therapy concerns itself with concrete goals that are achievable within a brief time period. The process of identifying the student's preferred future starts as soon as the student comes to the office and begins to take shape in response to the miracle question. Working with the counselor, the student will reshape this envisioned future into meaningful, concrete, achievable goals, characterized by each of the following (Berg & Miller, 1992, p. 32–44; De Jong & Miller, 1995, p. 730–731).

Goals: Important to the Student

During the initial stages of counseling, it is more important to engage the student as "customer" to identify what is important to him or her. The counselor's role is to truly encourage the student to take ownership of the goal and then, along with the student, embrace this goal as important. While this process is facilitated by the use of the miracle question format, some students may identify goals that they feel they should have or that the counselor may think is important, goals that are "socially" accepted or expected, rather than goals that are of real importance to them. When this appears to be the direction the student is taking, the counselor should invite the student to identify ways that achieving this goal would add value to his or her life. Questions as simple as, "What difference will this make in your life?" can help the student consider the value and take ownership of the goals identified.

If we return to the dialogue with Donna, we can see how the careful reflection and questioning of the counselor helped reframe the goal so that it truly had personal relevance and value to the student.

Counselor:	So, would anyone else notice?
Donna:	Yeah, Ashia and Mia, since I wouldn't be stoned getting on the bus, they would definitely notice.
Counselor:	Wow, so they would notice!
Donna:	That would blow their mind. And it would definitely throw Mrs. Howarth off her tracks, if I bounced into homeroom all cheery and focused and clearheaded and motivated.
Counselor:	Wow, that sounds like quite a miracle, quite a fantastic way to start your day, clearheaded, energetic, focused, motivated, and (laughing) with great breath!
Donna:	Yeah (laughing).
Counselor:	But seriously, you know it does sound nice, and this may sound a little strange, but I guess I'm wondering how would being clearheaded, energetic, focused be of value or use to you? You know, what difference would that make in your day or in you life?
Donna:	The first thing that came to my mind is yikes—I'd have to go to class straight—how boring!
Counselor:	Going to all your classes straight would be boring?
Donna:	Not really. I guess that's a cop out. Maybe if I wasn't so hung over and had some energy, I would understand what they were talking about and then maybe I would find it interesting.

Counselor: Maybe find it interesting? You mean your classes?

Donna: Well, I know I used to really like science and we are doing labs now and I used to really like them, but when I'm high I just goof around and then get in trouble. Maybe if I was clearheaded and focused I would have some fun doing the labs, like I used to.

Counselor: That's fantastic. So, one of the real goals would be to be clearheaded and focused and engage and enjoy your science labs.

Donna: Yeah, that would be cool.

In this simple exchange, the counselor was able to not only validate that this goal has personal value to the client, but also was able to reinforce that value for the client.

Goals: Small and Achievable

It is important for the counselor to help the student not only articulate a preferred future, but reframe this ultimate goal into smaller, achievable goals. The skilled counselor will help the student identify and then achieve a series of small goals—all of which contribute to the establishment of the bigger vision of the desired state. As noted by De Jong & Miller (1995), "It is easier to fill out a job application than to get a job" (p. 730). Setting and achieving small goals provides encouragement for the student's continued effort as well as offers markers against which the counselor and student can monitor progress.

If we briefly turn to the interaction the school counselor is having with Donna, this crafting of a goal so that it is small and achievable may simply take the form of asking the student to invest in just one mini-experiment.

Donna: Yeah, that would be cool.

Counselor: Yep. Sounds cool.

Donna: I'm going to do it . . . no more drugs, drinking . . . partying!

Counselor: Donna, I'm impressed by your enthusiasm, but how about if we start with tonight and tomorrow? What could you do tonight that would help you wake up on time, get out of bed, and start your day being pleasant and interacting with your mom?

Donna: Well, that should be easy. I'm scheduled to go to church choir tonight so I won't be hanging out.

Counselor: Great. So, if we get together tomorrow, we can see how much more energy and focus you have. That would be a super mini-experiment. What do you think?

Donna: Cool. I can see you at third period; that's my study hall and I have science class right before that!

Goals: Concrete and Behavioral

Berg and Miller (1992) say that nonbehavioral goals, such as having more self-esteem, living a sober lifestyle, and getting in touch with feelings are difficult to achieve, mainly because success and progress are difficult to gauge (p. 37). More than just difficult to gauge, they are also not easy to achieve and, as stated, they fail to provide directions on how to achieve them.

When inviting students to share their goals, it is not unusual for them to talk about what they want to have happen in vague and nonspecific ways. The solution-focused school counselor's job is to help students formulate specific, observable goals. Rather than working with goals that are vague and global statements of well-being, such as "I want to feel better," the effective school counselor helps the student redefine goals in concrete, specific, behavioral terms. Making goals concrete also facilitates their achievement. For example, the student who is referred because they are "bad" leaves the counselor little room for intervention. How exactly do we make a "bad" child, good? However, that same child, when presented as having difficulty sitting at his desk and doing his work, comes to the counselor with a vision of what the preferred future will look like. It is much easier for a counselor to facilitate movement from out-of-seat behavior to in-seat behavior than it is from moving the student from being bad to being good. So, the fourth grader who came to the office saying that his teacher wants him to stop being bad, may be asked questions such as, "What would that look like? What would you be doing when you were no longer being bad?" or "What will you be doing differently when you are good?" Hopefully these questions will elicit responses that are more concrete, specific, and action oriented. It is more useful for the counselor to work with this fourth grader if the goal is to "raise my hand before I call out an answer" or "wait until the teacher gives me permission to go to the pencil sharpener" than it is to help this student cease being bad.

If the student is unable to generate such a concrete framing of the goal, it is okay for the counselor to suggest options by presenting the student with possible multiple-choice answers (Cade & O'Hanlon, 1993).

For example, perhaps the counselor working with our fourth grader may ask, "When you are being good, will you be going to class every day, finishing assignments, telling your friends that you will see them after school, or perhaps something else?" The illustrations provided direct the student to think in terms of behavior and behavioral change.

Goals: Positive

Another characteristic of effective goals is that they are expressed as the presence of some behavior or some thing the student will be doing, rather than the absence of something (Berg & Miller, 1992). The student who states that he will no longer be in trouble needs to be helped to reframe this goal in a proactive, positive frame. In this case, the counselor may simply ask, "When you are no longer in trouble, what will you be doing instead?" Such a question may elicit a response such as, "I will be sitting in my seat doing the assigned deskwork." Reframing the original goal (i.e., no longer be in trouble) provides an observable marker and specific concrete target for change (i.e., sit in seat and do deskwork).

The following interaction between an elementary school counselor and Tony, a fifth-grade student, demonstrates how the school counselor not only reframed Tony's goals, making them more concrete and observable, but in the process also moved Tony to conceptualize goals in a positive frame (i.e., what he would be doing).

Counselor:	Tony, thanks for coming. I was wondering, if our work together is really successful, what do you think that would look like?
Tony:	Look like?
Counselor:	Well, what do you think would be different as a result of you and I working together?
Tony:	Oh, like, I wouldn't be getting in trouble any more and you know, like, things would be super!
Counselor:	Wow, that sounds exciting. So, things would be super. Things like?
Tony:	Well. . . . hmm . . . I wouldn't be in trouble in school and my parents wouldn't be on my case.
Counselor:	Okay. So, if you weren't in trouble in school and your parents were not on your case, that would make it super?
Tony:	Yeah.

Counselor: Good. But, I'm wondering, what would you be doing differently if you were no longer in trouble in school?

Tony: Well, I wouldn't be calling out in class or clowning around.

Counselor: I think I understand. But, if I was in class and I saw you now that things were "super," what would I see you doing, since now you weren't calling out or clowning around?

Tony: Just doin' my seatwork and raising my hand before calling out answers.

Counselor: Got it. So, we will know we are being successful when you are able to sit in your seat and do your seatwork. Oh yeah, and raise your hand to give an answer. This is what you meant by things would be super?

Tony: Yeah.

Goals: Scaled for Success

The solution-focused school counselor will attempt to help the student experience immediate success by taking the desired terminal goal—or the ideal as portrayed by the response to the miracle question—and break these down to smaller, more readily achievable goals. The process of goal scaling helps the student establish priorities for action and measure progress toward those markers.

The school counselor would explain the concept of a scale, labeled as "10" at one end for the desired goal in its full glory, and labeled "0" at the other end for the absence or lowest level of the possible presence of the desired goal. The student is then asked to rank his or her current experience (in reference to the desired goal) on this scale from $1 = $ low to $10 = $ high. For example, let's assume for one student, Jessica, the desired goal is to have a good group of friends that are close and would spend time on weekends together (10). The self-described 0 on this scale is being alone, only with family and having no peers as friends. When asked to place her current experience on this scale, Jessica noted she was at a 3.

It is important at this point to reiterate that the solution-focused counselor engages the student in his or her world. This takes form during the use of scaling in that the counselor does not engage in a debate about the accuracy or absolute validity of the student's self-assigned score. It is simply a reference from which the counselor and student will want to build. As such, the focus in not on "why" a 3, but rather the question focuses on what the student would need to do to move up a number on the scale.

Consider the following exchange between Jessica, a senior in high school, and her counselor, Mrs. Hayden.

Jessica: I guess I would say . . . about a 3.

Mrs. Hayden: Okay, so over here at 10, which we described as you having at least two very close girlfriends that you could trust with sharing the important things of your life. And here you are (pointing to a rough graph line) at a 3. Would you describe what a 3 looks like?

Jessica: Well. I seemed to be liked by people at school. I am "friends" with the girls on the newspaper, so I'm not a 0.

Mrs. Hayden: That's good. Now what would a 4 or a 5 look like?

Jessica: Hmm. I guess if, like, I had a couple of people I hung out with on weekends. You know, like went to the mall, or movies, or came over to my house and did something, just like someone I could call up and say hey let's go out.

Mrs. Hayden and Jessica both now have a clearer picture of what "progress" would look like, and they even have some data on the resources that Jessica brings to this situation. It is clear that Jessica has fundamental social skills and can engage her peers. The task for Mrs. Hayden and Jessica will be to creatively discover how these resources can be utilized to help Jessica move from a 3 up the scale to a 4 or 5.

The use of this scaling process can be very empowering to help make goals concrete and achievable, and empower the student to take responsibility for the change and the evaluation of his or her own progress. The scaling process also provides a structure for considering sequential steps that will bring the student closer to the ultimate goal. Thus, in subsequent sessions, the counselor and the student can review the scale and check where the student places him- or herself. If the student reports moving up the scale, it provides a focus for "investigating" what the student did to make this move and affirm the change taking place.

Mrs. Hayden: Well, Jessica, haven't seen you in two weeks—where would you place yourself on our magic scale?

Jessica: I'd say a 6 (smiling)!

Mrs. Hayden: Wow, a 6! What is it that let's you know you are at 6, as opposed to the 3?

Jessica:	Well, I was able to meet a couple of girls at the mall this past weekend, and I just saw Becky and Takia at lunch and asked them if they would want to come over tomorrow and they both said yes.
Mrs. Hayden:	Wow, that's fantastic. That really is movement up the scale.

The excitement and hopefulness is clear in Jessica's presentation and, with the counselor's support, they will begin to identify exactly how Jessica was able to make this movement. Identifying the specific behaviors, attitudes, and strategies employed will provide the raw materials for crafting a plan to make the move to the next level.

Goals: Requiring Hard Work

Change is difficult. As such, the solution-focused school counselor helps the student accept that goal achievement involves "hard work" and doesn't immediately and consistently occur. This should not be a surprise nor a new concept for the student. The student has worked "hard" at learning to ride a bike, or play a sport or musical instrument, or even learn a video game—hard doesn't mean painful, it does however mean involving concerted effort. Let's return to the dialogue with Tony.

Tony:	Just doin' my seatwork and raising my hand before calling out answers.
Counselor:	Got it. So, we will know we are being successful when you are able to sit in your seat and do your seatwork. Oh yeah, and raise your hand to give an answer. This is what you meant by things would be super?
Tony:	Yeah. But I am not good at keepin' quiet.
Counselor:	Well, in some ways, we don't want you to keep quiet. I mean, you really have good ideas and they are worth sharing in the class. I guess what we have to figure out is how to help you raise your hand first, and then share what you are thinking?
Tony:	Yeah, that's what Mr. Lansen says—I'm smart but I interrupt.
Counselor:	Okay, that's good. So, we have to put our heads together and try to come up with some ideas that will help you remember to raise your hand before giving an answer?
Tony:	But what happens if it doesn't work?

Counselor: I guess if what we decide doesn't work, then we both will be disappointed. But then maybe we could think about it, and figure out how to improve. Whew! That sounds like we are these fancy scientists—thinking about something, then trying it and then analyzing it and then redoing it . . .

Tony: I like that kind of stuff . . .

Counselor: Well, that's great. So, we are really going to need you to not only try our plans out, but then also be able to help me understand what really worked well and what needs to be improved upon.

Focusing on the work that needs to be done not only empowers the student as being personally responsible for the achievement of the goal, but also allows for some face saving should he or she initially fall short of goal achievement. Everyone falls off the bike in the beginning, or gets confused using the various game buttons. Even those who we hold up as models of success have histories of monumental failure. Babe Ruth once held not only the record for most homeruns in a season, but the most strikeouts as well.

The fact is that change is difficult, and there will be setbacks, but the successful person is one who preservers. Slow, steady progress can be accepted as normal and the client can be praised for the hard work (Berg & Miller, 1992, p. 42).

WHAT'S NEXT?

With goals clearly identified and scaled, and resources identified from analyses of coping skills and exceptions, the counselor and student are now poised to focus their discourse on the design, implementation, and monitoring of realistic plans for achievement of the student's goals. The strategies employed during this phase of the counseling process are discussed in Chapter 5.

SUMMARY

Change Discourse

- The processes grouped under the rubric of "solution discourse" all serve as intermediate interventions that help the student connect his or her current change processes with strategies that will be employed to obtain his or her goals.

Collaborative Relationship

- The solution-focused school counselor employs all the core elements found in all effective counseling. In addition to the core conditions of warmth, genuineness, and unconditional positive regard, the solution-focused school counselor employs encouragement, compliments, and affirmations as the counselor and student together identify and embrace the student's goals.

Miracle Question

- As defined by Berg & Miller (1992), the miracle question is a "[. . .] specially designed interview process . . . [which] orients the client away from the past and the problem and toward the future and a solution" (p. 13).
- The miracle question is simply a future oriented question that invites the student to envision a future time when he or she and his or her world are exactly as they wish it to be. This future-oriented question is useful with goal setting since it shifts the focus from problems and their genesis to the unlimited range of possibilities when envisioning a preferred future.

Goal Setting and Working With Goals

- Working with the counselor, the student will reshape this envisioned future into meaningful, concrete, achievable goals, characterized by each of the following:

  1. Engage the student as "customer" to identify what is important to him or her.
  2. Reframe the ultimate goal into smaller, achievable goals thus providing encouragement for the student's continued effort, as well as offering markers against which the counselor and student can monitor progress.
  3. Help students formulate specific, observable goals. Rather than working with goals that are vague and global statements of well-being, such as "I want to feel better," the solution-focused school counselor helps the student redefine his or her goals in concrete, specific, behavioral terms. Making goals concrete also facilitates their achievement.

(Continued)

(Continued)

4. Express goals as the presence of some behavior or something the student will be doing, rather than the absence of something.

5. Scale the ideal as portrayed by the response to the miracle question, and break these down to smaller, more readily achievable goals. The process of goal scaling helps the student establish priorities for action and measure progress toward those markers.

6. Accept and help the student understand that goal achievement involves "hard work" and doesn't immediately and consistently occur.

Identifying and Implementing Goal-Attainment Strategies

5

I t is important to note that while presented here as the "third" form of discourse, once again, some neat and orderly sequence to this process does not reflect the real-world experience of the school counselor. In the real world, the counselor and student are engaged in a dynamic exchange that goes in and out of all three forms of discourse. The plans and strategies developed and employed during strategy discourse will be continuously revised as the working relationship changes and the focus of the preferred future emerges with increased clarity.

The school counselor operating from a solution-focused framework is interested in identifying strategies that have served the student well at other times and circumstances, even if these strategies were devalued and underutilized. As previously noted, this is a departure from more traditional approaches that often engage the counselor in the development of complicated interventions that require a rewiring of the student in an attempt to "fix" what is broken. This shift in paradigm is significant and needs to be highlighted. With this as the looking glass to process student data through, the school counselor with a solution-focused orientation relinquishes the role of problem solver, behavioral programmer, or even fundamental "interventionist," and steps into the facilitative role of collaborator, attempting to generalize previous strengths and success strategies to the current situation.

The specific elements of solution discourse leading to the identification and implementation of goal-attainment strategies include: (1) using the language of change, (2) identifying and employing student strengths,

(3) working with exceptions, (4) externalizing the problem, and (5) developing specific tasks.

USING LANGUAGE OF CHANGE

Embracing a constructivist perspective, solution-focused school counselors use encouragement and affirmation to create and maintain a hope-filled, positive orientation to working with the student. As most school counselors have experienced, students often present at the counselor's office beaten down and believing that nothing will help. Helping a student find evidence of his or her resources and successes sets the stage for that student coming to believe that this track record of successful coping bodes well for future success. The counselor's efforts are geared to a reframing—focusing on strength and resources—that, in turn, helps the student become more hopeful and less resigned to remaining stuck in this problem state.

One strategy particularly effective when used with the discouraged student is for the counselor to share his or her own surprise and curiosity about how the student has managed to hang on, to cope, in the face of such diversity. This is not a ploy, or a game, or a gimmick. For the solution-focused counselor who is able to join the student in his or her world, the constructed reality of living with, and in, this "huge" problem allows the counselor to truly be surprised and even in awe that the student is coping as well as he or she is.

Coping Questions

Rather than engaging the student in a listing of all his or her limitations and failures, the counselor can use a "coping question" such as, "How have you managed so far?" or "How have you prevented the problem from getting worse?" to redirect the student to focus on his or her strengths and resources. The counselor's use of a coping question gently challenges the student's sense of hopelessness and highlights the resources the student brings to the current situation. This strategy was employed by Alex, a middle school counselor working with Jamie, who was referred to the counselor's office because of cutting classes.

Jamie: I hate school and don't want to be here.

Counselor: I understand you don't like school, but it looks like somehow you haven't cut English class once this marking period. Wow. How do you do that?

Jamie: I don't know. I like what we are talking about in that class and the teacher seems to like me.

Jamie's initial disclosure of hating school was certainly an invitation to pursue the when and why of this condition. But that discussion would have only unearthed "problems" and even reinforced Jamie's construct of school as hate-able. In this situation, the counselor's use of the coping question helped to refocus Jamie away from a rigid, problem stance to the realization that exceptions to this problematic situation do exist. Simply identifying that she is, in fact, capable of remaining in class frames that as an ability, a strength, and a resource that can be affirmed and perhaps employed. This refocusing on strengths and resources provides a spring-board from which to engage in solution talk.

Words of Encouragement

In addition to using coping questions, the solution-focused counselor is mindful of the power specific words have in supporting a construct of hope and encouraging and empowering the student to invest in change strategies. The words employed construct a vision of a future in which change has occurred and the problem no longer exists.

Thus, when a student provides evidence that runs contrary to their "problem," as was the case with Jamie's attendance in English class, the counselor is quick to affirm this. Yet, often upon receiving such affirmation for this "exception," the student may quickly retreat to the problem construct by dismissing this exception as a fluke, or simply happenstance. Under these conditions, the counselor needs to encourage the student to revisit the decisions he or she made to create this exception, and then affirm that ability and strength. This affirmation turns attention back to the student, rather than the experience, and highlights the stability of these personal resources. This may take the form of a validating and reinforcing statement such as, "Wow, that sounds wonderful. How did you make that happen?" Once the "exception" is framed as a consequence of the student's use of his or her own resource, the student will be unable to discount it as a fluke, or a once in a lifetime occurrence.

Language of the Future

Even the "tense" of the language used in session has importance to the solution-focused counselor. When students present the problem as ever present, the school counselor will attempt to reframe that description as a historic experience that we do not need to carry into the future. For example, hearing phrases such as, "I'm always in trouble" or "I'm always skipping class," the solution-focused school counselor is quick to change the tense of the language to indicate that was then, and we have a now and a future that we can still affect. Upon hearing the above disclosures the solution-focused counselor may respond: "Oh, so *you've been* in trouble," or "So you *were* skipping . . ." While this shift in verb tense may appear extremely subtle, it is a shift of significance to the process of reconstructing a vision, a belief of a hopeful future. The shift in verb tense sets the stage for viewing the problem as in the past, thus allowing for a sense of optimism about the present and future condition.

Hopeful Tone

Another element important to the construction of a working relationship conducive for change is the use of hopeful tones throughout the discourse. Employing a definitive tone rather than language of possibility expresses the counselor's expectation that positive change will occur. Thus, rather than constructing a vision of a future based on "if" (e.g., "If you are able to complete the assignment, then . . ."), the solution-focused school counselor employs more definitive tones with phrases such as, "*When* you complete the assignment, then . . ." Setting such a definitive tone encourages the student to believe that a preferred future is achievable.

The importance of language and conversation as the source of constructed realities cannot be overstated. The solution-focused school counselor needs to be alert to opportunities to employ encouraging and change-maintaining conversation. Table 5.1 provides a number of illustrations of how these conversations may look.

FOCUSING ON STRENGTHS

Fundamental to the solution-focused approach is the attention and focus given to the identification and employment of the student's existing strengths and resources rather than on what the student lacks (Berg, 1994; Durrant, 1995). School counselors with a solution-focused orientation value the fact that students have talents, resources, abilities, and strengths that have allowed them to advance to this point. At very basic levels, the students with whom we work—all of the students—have demonstrated competence and the ability to succeed. While these abilities and the resulting success may not be immediately evident in their current schoolwork, the challenge for the school counselor is to help the student identify and articulate those successful experiences and the strengths and abilities that led to them, even when these experiences lie outside the academic arena. Resources the student has employed in school to find some success, or outside of school to successfully navigate through life, can serve as the essential ingredients to a solution for the present concern.

Consider the student labeled as having a conduct problem. While the student may be acting out in class and causing disruption for the teacher,

Table 5.1   Conversations Encouraging and Maintaining Change

Questions/Reflections of Encouragement

- How did you do that (success)?
- What will be a small sign you are heading toward your goal?
- What is the easiest, smallest step you can take toward your goal?
- What will you need to do to take a small step toward your goal?
- What will you need to do to increase exceptions/decrease problems?
- What has changed since last we met (or since making the appointment)?
- How have you coped to this point?

Questions/Reflections Maintaining Change

- What have you noticed that's different?
- Where do you see yourself now on our scale?
- What will you need to do to keep the changes going?
- How will you know when it is time to get back on track? (or that you are starting to slide?)
- What will you need to do to get back on track?
- What difference will that make?
- What have others noticed or said about . . . ?

this same student may be a contributing member of a sports team or a band, or perhaps show leadership capabilities even when these have been employed to the dismay of his teachers. The solution-focused counselor values these successes and in session will attempt to identify and clarify how the student achieved success at these times. For example, the same student referred to the office for "fighting" or "flipping out in the classroom" may be a successful athlete who restrains from acting that way in a game. Working with this student, the counselor would be very interested in identifying the resources the student employs during the game that help him or her control the behavior. A question such as, "How did you stay calm when she (the other team member) fouled you?" or, "How did you resist retaliating when the guy blocked you in the back after the whistle had blown?" will help identify strengths and resources the student brings to the counseling. Or, consider the student who has a difficult time engaging in cooperative learning exercises in the classroom, yet is a successful member of a band. Working with this student, the solution-focused counselor will be eager to understand how it is possible for the student to contribute ideas about the music *and* embrace the ideas of the others in the band, so as to make a song they all really like. The ability of our student to restrain from fighting in a game and/or creatively cooperating with fellow band members is a resource, a strength, that once identified can be engaged to facilitate movement up the scale toward the student's preferred future. This process is illustrated in the brief exchange between Shannon and her counselor, Mrs. Wicks.

Mrs. Wicks: Shannon, you appear to really have a large group of friends.

Shannon: Yeah, my girls.

Mrs. Wicks: Your girls?

Shannon: Yeah, like we have this "sorority" and I'm kind of the leader.

Mrs. Wicks: Wow! How were you able to get them to follow you and your ideas? That's cool . . . (smiling) kind of a "natural-born leader"?

Shannon: I guess. I just seem to have some good ideas and I can get them to agree.

Mrs. Wicks: That's quite a skill. You are creative, coming up with good ideas, then you also know how to convince them your ideas are good?

Shannon: Yeah. I don't know, just seems kind of easy and I like the things we do.

Mrs. Wicks: Easy for you—not everyone can be creative or persuasive. When was the last time you can remember using that creativity and skills of persuasion in class?

Shannon: Huh?

Mrs. Wicks: Well, I am sure you don't leave your creativity or your ability to explain your point of view, or your ideas, at home. So, have you ever had a situation where you worked with other students on a project, or something like that, and convinced them to do it the way you wanted?

Shannon: Do you mean, like in social studies, when we would debate? I liked that. I was pretty good.

Mrs. Wicks: I bet you were. I am wondering, how did you do that? You know, participate in class and enjoy it?

Having identified Shannon's strengths, Mrs. Wicks will now want to understand a bit more about Shannon's exception (to her disruptive classroom behavior) that is evident in her successful use of her ability to be creative and persuasive as demonstrated in social studies class debates.

Identifying how Shannon was able to engage these strengths in that setting sets the stage for planning on using these strengths in a prosocial, proacademic manner.

WORKING WITH EXCEPTIONS

Even students who appear to be totally immersed in a problematic life have had experiences when the problem or the concerns were nonexistent, or present in a weaker form. This realization directs the solution-focused school counselor to identify and then amplify these "exceptions" to the current situation. The solution-focused counselor, engaging in strategy discourse, is attentive to opportunities to clarify times, contexts, and conditions when the student's problem was either not a problem or less of one (Berg, 1994; Cade & O'Hanlon, 1993). Finding these "exceptions" is truly like finding a gold mine. The exceptions, once understood, can provide the student with a blueprint that, if followed, can move the student closer to his or her goal and in so doing solve the problem.

The basic format for exception questions is something like, "Can you think of a time in the past [time period] that you did not have a problem with . . . ?" By asking the student *exception-finding questions* the counselor helps the student locate and appreciate moments in the past when the current problem got handled. For a child who feels as if she is "always in trouble," locating a day or a class or an activity during which she was successful—not reprimanded—stimulates hope that this experience is possible and that things are not so hopeless and absolute. While a generic question such as, "Is there a time when this problem does not occur or occurs less than at other times?" can be useful, for some students it may be easier if the question is more specific and focused. Questions such as, "When are you able to raise your hand before answering?" or "When was the last time you were able to get your assignment in on time?" narrow down the search in hopes of finding strengths and resources that are directly applicable to the current concern.

In presenting the exception question it is helpful to employ "positive" language pointing to success, as opposed to words that highlight the problem (O'Hanlon & Weiner-Davis, 1989). Thus, asking the student to "Tell me about a time when you ignored and walked away from another student's taunt" may be more effective and hope-filled than a question such as, "Is there ever a time that you were able to walk away from another student's taunt?" The variation is subtle, but may be significant in creating a mindset suggesting that the counselor believes this student has been successful and can be again.

While, on first review, it may be simple enough to ask a student, "Could you tell me about a time when this was not a problem or it wasn't as big of a problem as it is now?" the value in identifying exception rests in the in-depth analyses of these exceptions. It is important to understand the specifics that contributed to each exception. How did the student get this to happen? What specific cognitions, feelings, behaviors, and social supports were engaged to bring this exception into fruition?

Detailing of the specifics of who, what, when, where, and perhaps most importantly, how that led to the creation of this exception allows the elements of a successful solution to emerge. The counselor, upon hearing the exception, wants to highlight the specifics so that they can be crafted into a useful solution plan and thus may follow up the exception question with a sequence of questions such as:

"How did you get that to happen?"

"What's different about those times?"

"What did you do differently?"

"How would you explain this success? These differences?"

"How could more of that happen?"

Of special note is the "tone" of these questions. Rather than assuming that the exception was a fluke of nature or an accident, the questions suggest that this exception was a result of the deliberate action on the part of the student. Believing that it was within his or her power to affect this exception encourages the student to believe that similar deliberate actions can be carried out with the same result.

In reviewing the following vignette regarding Jessica, we can see how the counselor employed exception analyses to help her move up the scale.

Mrs. Hayden:	Okay. So Jessica, you see yourself at a 3, and a 4 or 5 would be when you are able to socialize with a couple of girls at your house or at the mall.
Jessica:	Yeah, that would be nice.
Mrs. Hayden:	I am wondering, was there ever a time when you did do something with a couple of girls?
Jessica:	Even like schoolwork?
Mrs. Hayden:	Sure.
Jessica:	Hmm. Last week, I asked a couple of the girls on the newspaper if they wanted to get together at my house on the weekend and do the layout for this issue.

Mrs. Hayden: Perfect. How did you do that?

Jessica: Do what?

Mrs. Hayden: Well, you actually did something that you said you wanted to do to move up your scale. You invited these girls over. How did you do that? How did you decide to invite them? How did you get the confidence to invite them?

Jessica: Oh, I see. I don't know. It didn't seem like a big deal since I knew they were into the paper, and I was just asking if they wanted to work on it with me, and if they said no, it was not a big deal cause we would just do it during the week.

Mrs. Hayden: Okay. So, I understand. The fact that you knew they were into the paper, and you believed that if they said no, that while that may be disappointing, it wasn't a major upset?

Jessica: Yeah. I felt pretty comfortable asking.

Mrs. Hayden: That's super. It seems that when you have an idea about something that may interest another group of girls and you can be comfortable with them saying no thanks, then you seem to be able to actually invite them to do something with you, which is what you described as a 4 on your scale.

Assuming Jessica agrees with Mrs. Hayden's analysis, the two of them would begin to strategize on how to use these same skills/attitudes (i.e., picking something of interest to others, and being comfortable with a "no, thank you") to invite some students to do something other than schoolwork.

Up to this point, the illustrations suggest that exception finding typically targets the student's "ancient history" of success. As sessions continue, the experiences of success that may have occurred between sessions also provide a source for tweaking or recreating the intervention. This can be as specific as asking the student to investigate any changes or improvements that may have happened in the time between being referred and coming to the office for the first session. For example, a student who had been asked to leave class because of a temper outburst may enter the office upset, and even agitated, but perhaps more in control than he had previously been in the classroom. This shift in behavior from the problem state (temper outburst) to a more desired state (angry yet in control) has been termed "pre-session change" (O'Hanlon & Weiner-Davies, 1989). Analyzing how this student was able to gain this level of control could provide meaningful data that can be used and generalized to the classroom experience.

Indentifying Exceptions When Not Easily Identified

Identifying exceptions is not always a smooth and easy process. It is possible that a student may be unable to identify a time when the "problem" did not exist. Under these conditions, the counselor wants to help the student by refocusing on times when the problem situation was not as severe or intense (O'Hanlon & Weiner-Davis, 1989). Identifying times when the problem situation is not as severe again provides the counselor and the student the opportunity to drill down and identify what it was that the client was doing, feeling, and believing that resulted in the more positive situation.

For example, consider the situation in which a student who gets anxious each time she is asked to speak in front of the class is able to identify a time when she was less nervous—less anxious. Understanding this exception would become the focus for the student-counselor discourse. Through their discourse and analysis of this exception, the counselor and student identify a couple of elements that seem to help the student feel less anxious in this particular situation. The first element is that the presentation was on a topic she really enjoyed—her hobby of model building. She also had a visual aid (a ship in a bottle) and all of the kids in class seemed to be looking at it and not her. A final element is that the class was really engaged—not sitting quietly—but actively asking questions. The client in this situation felt like the expert and enjoyed sharing her knowledge. While the student was not at a 10 in terms of her level of relaxation, she was more relaxed than in similar situations when she has to make a classroom presentation. The counselor and student will attempt to identify how these elements helped reduce the anxiety and begin to craft these into intervention strategies. Assuming the essential element is that the topic was something she liked and felt confident in discussing, the counselor and student may craft the following intervention. The plan for approaching the next presentation is to (1) choose topics of interest and (2) really prepare so that she becomes the "resident expert."

Looking for Exceptions With a Defensive Student

Another challenge that may be experienced by the school counselor seeking to find exceptions is that a child—feeling defensive or perhaps simply beaten down—is unable to find and report a time of any level of success. Under these conditions, it sometimes helps to reframe the question to elicit a response as if from another's perspective. For example, "Suppose I ask your parents whether you have had any better days recently. What would they say?" Assuming the child is able to describe the situation from this perspective, the counselor would attempt to gently follow-up by seeking details that would help both the student and counselor understand the "who, what, when, and where" of this exception. This was the case that Ms. Pesanie experienced while working with Louie, a second-grade student who was reported being aggressive and pushing his classmates.

Ms. Pesanie:	So Louie, it seems that you get into this "problem" of pushing your classmates when it's time to line up for lunch?
Louie:	I guess.
Ms. Pesanie:	Can you tell me about a time when you got in the lunch line and didn't push your classmates?
Louie:	No . . .
Ms. Pesanie:	Well, I'm wondering, if your mom and dad were here, what would they say are times when you can stand in a line, and wait without pushing?
Louie	I don't know.
Ms. Pesanie:	Well, let's pretend they are here . . . right over there . . . and I say . . . "Hi Mr. and Mrs. Z. Louie and I are trying to remember a time or place when Louie had to get into a line and he was really very patient and cooperative and simply waiting his turn." Let's pretend. What do you think they may say?
Louie:	Maybe they would say that the other day I stood in line waiting for ice cream. We had to wait in a long line and I did that without pushing.
Ms. Pesanie:	Perfect! That's exactly what I was looking for; that's a super example of a time when this problem didn't exist! Thank you, Mr. and Mrs. Z (smiling).

Attributing Success to Another

One final challenge in working with exceptions is when the counselor works with a student who, while identifying exceptions, places the power and responsibility for these exceptions on to another, rather than on what he or she did differently. For example, the student identifying a time when he didn't get in trouble in English class noted that, "The teacher was just in a good mood—I didn't do anything differently—she just didn't get on my case." In this situation, the counselor still wants to turn the attention back to the student as a means of giving that student the control. Perhaps asking the student to describe how he acts when the teacher is in a good mood may unveil some characteristics—some behaviors that they could experiment with prior to knowing if the teacher is in a good mood.

Maurice: She was just in a good mood and wasn't on my case.

Counselor: Okay. But if I was in class on one of these days that she is in a good mood, what would I notice you doing?

Maurice: I don't know. I just sit there. I'm kind of relaxed, I guess.

Counselor: That's good. What else would you be doing besides sitting being relaxed?

Maurice: I don't know. When she's not on my case, I don't mind participating in class.

Counselor: So, if I was observing the class and could tell she was in a good mood, I would also notice that you appear relaxed and are participating in class activities.

Maurice: That sounds right.

Perhaps, if Maurice would be willing to try to include these elements (i.e., relaxing and participating) in his next class, he (and the counselor) may discover that these behaviors help contribute to the teacher's good mood or even if not, perhaps these behaviors may still help to keep Maurice out of trouble even if the teacher is in a bad mood.

EXTERNALIZING THE PROBLEM

An extension of exception finding is the use of an approach called "externalizing the problem" (White & Epston, 1990). This is a process in which the counselor reframes the problem as something outside of the client. For example, a student who bends under social pressure from peers, or flips out because the person next to them bugs him or her, is externalizing the problem. The counselor working with a student and the externalized problem will attempt to engage the student in identifying the degree to which he or she feels influence over the problem. For example, the counselor may ask, "So, when all of your friends are pressuring you to cut class with them, are there times when you have power to resist?" or "When was the last time that you were able to say no to their pressure?"

If we allow the student to externalize the problem, then we may be able to engage him or her in a dialogue about ways the pesky situations were resisted in the past. If the student responds, "I didn't go drinking 'cause I told them my dad would kill me," or "I couldn't cut class because I wouldn't be able to play in the game that night," the counselor affirms these as illustrations of the power the student has over these "externalized problems." The key is to empower the students, helping them recognize that they are not "victims" and that they have resisted these externalized problems.

A slight modification of this externalization process has been presented by Berg (1994), suggesting that rather than blaming the students for their shortcomings or lack of trying, the counselor could/should blame the problem. So that rather than asking, "Why didn't they assert themselves and say 'no' to their friends?" the counselor may ask, "When does the pressure of being like your friends make you give into it?" This question helps reduce the sense of failure and also sets the stage for identifying times when the pressure of being like their friends was resisted.

DEVELOPING TASKS

A significant element to strategy discourse is engaging the student in the identification and application of a small task that will move the student closer to his or her goal. The solution-focused school counselor, in ending a session, would summarize the strengths and resources identified in session and compliment the student for all the good work he or she did in identifying strategies for moving closer to the goal. Following this summary, the counselor would then invite the student to identify a specific task that he or she could try before the next session. The counselor might ask the student, "What one small thing could you try that may move you closer to your goal?" or perhaps the counselor would more directly suggest, "I wonder what would happen if you . . . ?" The goal of this "task development" is to move the student away from simply thinking about and discussing small steps to engaging in steps toward solving the problem. Engaging the student in specific steps—specific actions—helps target a well-thought plan and begins the process of assimilating this plan into the student's repertoire of available responses to the problematic situation.

An example might be in the case of the counselor working with Louie (the patient person in the ice cream line). The counselor may ask Louie, as homework, to act like a mini-scientist and simply gather some data.

Counselor: Louie, would you be willing to do a little project for me? It's going to be hard and it will require you to eat some ice cream (smiling).

Louie: Project?

Counselor: How about if I ask your mom and dad to take you out to have ice cream after dinner some night?

Louie: I like that project.

Counselor: Well, that's the easy part. Here's what I want you to do. When you go for ice cream and there is a line that you have to wait in, I want you to remember what you are doing or thinking when you stand in line. Could you do that?

Louie: You mean just like if I'm talking to my mom or looking at the pictures of the ice cream stuff, just remember that?

Counselor: Yep, that's perfect. If you could do that, then you and I could talk about it and see how it helped you to stay calm in line.

Louie: Okay, I can do that.

This "homework" would then be discussed in the upcoming session and whatever data Louie was able to gather would be analyzed to provide valuable information for further strategy formation for use in the lunch line.

SUMMARY

Strategy Discourse

- The plans and strategies developed and employed during strategy discourse will be continuously revised as the working relationship changes and the focus of the preferred future emerges with increased clarity.
- The specific elements of solution discourse leading to the identification and implementation of goal attainment strategies include: (1) using the language of change, (2) identifying and employing student strengths, (3) working with exceptions, (4) externalizing the problem, and (5) developing specific tasks.

Using Language of Change

- Embracing a constructivist perspective, solution-focused school counselors are mindful of, and attentive to, opportunities to employ encouragement and affirmation to facilitate the creation and maintenance of a hope-filled, positive orientation to working with the student.
- Rather than engaging the student in a listing of all his or her limitations and failures, the counselor can use a "coping question" such as, "How have you managed so far?" or "How have you prevented the problem from getting worse?" to redirect the student to focus on his or her strengths and resources.
- Even the verb tense is important with solution-focused counselors employing future and present tense rather than past tense.

The shift in verb tense sets the stage for viewing the problem as in the past, thus allowing for a sense of optimism about the present and future condition.

Focusing on Strengths

- Fundamental to the solution-focused approach is the attention and focus given to the identification and employment of the student's existing strengths and resources, rather than on what the student lacks.

Working With Exceptions

- The solution-focused counselor, engaging in strategy discourse, is attentive to opportunities to clarify times, contexts, and conditions when the student's problem was either not a problem or less of one.
- The exceptions, once understood, can provide the student with a blueprint that, if followed, can move the student closer to the goal and in so doing solve the problem.

Externalizing the Problem

- This is a process in which the counselor reframes the problem as something outside of the client.
- The counselor working with a student and the externalized problem will attempt to engage the student in identifying the degree to which he or she feels can influence the problem.
- The key is to empower the students, helping them recognize that they are not "victims" and that they have resisted these externalized problems.

Developing Tasks

- A significant element to strategy discourse is engaging the student in the identification and application of a small task that will move him or her closer to his or her goal.
- The goal of this "task development" is to move the student away from simply thinking about and discussing small steps to engaging in steps toward solving the problem.

Part III

From the Eyes of the Solution-Focused Expert

Pepinsky and Pepinsky (1954) recognized that if counseling is considered, in part, a cognitive activity, then the process of becoming a counselor must involve the acquisition of cognitive skills, and not just behavioral skills of social interaction. While the principles, constructs, and strategies of a solution-focused approach to school counseling has been the focus of this text, the purpose is to assist you in the process of "thinking" like a solution-focused school counselor.

A review of the literature identifying differences between "expert" and "novice" professionals points to the fact that those with expertise encode, organize, and use client information much differently than those new to the profession. Rather than organizing client data into categories that are based on superficial, irrelevant cues that may not be pertinent to generating a problem solution, experts have organizational cognitive structures, schemas, that help them quickly make sense of the information that a client presents. The employment of a solution-focused orienting framework facilitates the school counselor's ability to store client data in problem-relevant categories that are connected by underlying conceptual principles relevant to a problem solution, a process which is highly characteristic of those identified as "experts" (Chi, Feltovich, & Glaser, 1981).

In addition to the ability to discern the relevant from the irrelevant and to store these data efficiently, the effective school counselor uses procedural knowledge to guide his or her interactions in session. The effective counselor reflects "on" and "in" session, approaching each encounter by organizing client data into "If [condition phase], then [action phase]" statements. The effective counselor is alert to what the client presents (i.e., the "if") and is ready to respond (i.e., the "then") in ways that maximize effectiveness.

Developing procedural knowledge requires that we move beyond simply understanding solution-focused concepts and constructs, and begin to practice their application. The final two chapters are designed to support the development of this procedural thinking. In Chapter 6, you are provided an in-depth look at solution-focused school counselors in action. While the cases illustrate the use of specific solution-focused "strategies," the value in reviewing these case illustrations is the insight offered into the thinking of the solution-focused counselors as they process student information and make decisions "in" and "on" their practice. Chapter 7 invites you to vicariously step into the decision-making process, offering two cases illustrating the application of a solution-focused model. In Chapter 7, the reader is invited to employ the lens of a solution-focused counselor to process the student's information and to decide on the intervention he or she would employ at specific points in the session. The reader is then introduced to the thinking of the counselor in the illustration and the specific translation of that thinking into action as reflected in the next segment of dialogue.

Before we proceed, one caveat is in order. Textbook cases like those presented within this book, while based on composites of real students and real counseling sessions, have been sanitized to fit neatly into the confines of a book page. As you are more than aware, each student and each interaction is unique and does not follow the nice, sequential script of a textbook. However, even with that as a caveat, the cases to follow will allow you to set the targets—identify the markers—and clearly have your thinking and your practice take on the shape of a solution-focused school counselor.

Solution-Focused School Counselor **6**

Reflecting "in" and "on" Practice

As noted in the preface, the primary focus for this text, and all of the texts in this series, is the development of the school counselor's ability to translate theory into practice as evidenced by way of reflection "in" and "on" practice. The current chapter invites you to begin the process of using a solution-focused orientation as the filter through which to interpret student data and to begin to devise intervention strategies. The current chapter provides three case illustrations of school counselors employing a solution-focused orienting model to guide their reflections "on" and "in" session. It is suggested that as you review each of the cases you attempt to use your understanding of solution-focused orienting model to anticipate the counselors' thinking and subsequent action. It is in anticipating the counselors' thoughts and actions that you will also employ procedural knowledge from a solution-focused orientation, thus "thinking" like the expert!

In the first case, the solution-focused counselor illustrates his reflections "in" session that guided him as he allowed the client to focus on the problem, while gently inviting her to move from this "problem" talk to engage in "goal-speak" and initial goal scaling. The second case illustrates the counselor's ability to move the student from being a "complainant" to being a "customer." The final case provides a complete overview of the counselor's reflection "in" and "on" practice as counselor and client transition from the initial contact and saying "hello" to termination and the process of saying "goodbye."

CASE 1: NIKITA

Relating First, Resolving Later

Reflection "on" Practice

Dr. Zhang, Nikita's twelfth-grade counselor, was aware that Nikita would be returning to school this day, following a two-week absence. Niki's father and younger brother were tragically killed by a drunk driver and Niki is immersed in the grieving process. Thinking about what this young woman has been going through and anticipating the possible impact it could have on her own vision of a future, and her ability to come back to school, set the stage for Dr. Zhang's request to see Niki.

Operating from a solution-focused orienting model, Dr. Zhang's first-session goals included:

1. The formation of a collaborative relationship.

2. The creation of a climate for change.

3. Clarification of the goals of counseling.

4. Unearthing Niki's resources and strengths.

5. Exploration of tasks.

While approaching the session with the aforementioned goals in mind, Dr. Zhang was aware that the direction of the session would be set by Niki and not his preset goals.

Reflection "in" Practice

Creating a Collaborative Relationship

I entered the relationship valuing the need to create a supportive, collaborative relationship. Nikita has had her life turned upside down. In her grieving, she needs affirmation that what she is experiencing is "normal" and that there is a light at the end of the process. However, I need to be sensitive to her needs and thus must really be attentive and empathic, validating and acknowledging her experiences.

Dr. Z: Good morning, Niki. Thank you for coming down.

Niki: Hi.

Dr. Z: First of all, I want to tell you how very sorry I am for your loss and I am wondering how you are doing?

Niki: Okay, I guess—it's just really hard.

Dr. Z: I bet it was and is really hard.

Niki: Yeah (tearing), I know people are all trying to help but I couldn't get into the front door without everybody telling me how sorry they were and asking me if I am okay. Crap! I don't know if I'm okay—my dad and brother died.

Dr. Z: All of us who care about you are at a loss of what to say or do. We can't understand all that you are going through. In fact, it sounds like there are times when you are not sure what you are going through or how well you are doing.

Niki: It's just so hard (crying). Why did all of this have to happen? My poor mom. I don't think I should be here.

Dr. Z: There is a lot your mom and you are trying to work through. I can't imagine how hard it must be and truly I am amazed at your ability to push yourself to come to school.

Reflection "in" Practice

While I want to begin to identify goals and resources, I need to be sensitive to Niki's needs.

Niki: I did it for my mom. I could care less about school. What's the difference? You set all of these plans up and then some drunk wipes them away.

Reflection "in" Practice

I was hoping to have Niki shift her focus to look at her strength to move forward in life. She was able to get herself to school and if we could identify how she did that, we may be able to use that as motivation for reengaging in her studies. But it is clear that she is very sad, angry, and may need to vent about this within a safe, nonjudgmental setting.

Dr. Z: It feels like all of your plans have been wiped clean?

Niki: Really! Why give a damn about proms, senior day—stupid things. What do they really matter?

Dr. Z: I guess that proms and typical senior activities just don't seem important when you go through what you are going through.

Niki: I don't know why I'm here.

Dr. Z: If I understand you, you came today because you felt it was something your mom wanted?

(Continued)

(Continued)

Niki: Yeah. She really wants me to get back to my life. But what life? It feels so horrible.

Dr. Z: Niki, it is horrible. It is horrible to lose two people you love. But your mom must feel that you can and should try to reengage in your life.

Reflection "in" Practice

Creating a Climate for Change

I would like to create a climate for change. I would like to help Niki see that things not only can be different, but actually are starting to be different than the all-engulfing pain and grief experienced over the past two weeks.

Niki: She said it's okay to be sad, but we will survive and that dad and Thomas would want us to get on with our lives. But it's hard. I just don't feel like it. I feel angry at people here who are going around like life is a blast. It isn't; it sucks!

Dr. Z: I think I can understand how hopeless it may seem, but I am amazed that with all the sadness you feel, and even the anger at your classmates for not understanding what it is like to be you, that you still were able to come to school. That's truly amazing. How did you do that?

Reflection "in" Practice

I was hoping to get Niki to begin to see her strengths—her coping skills— and that change is possible.

Niki: I don't know. I just did it for my mom.

Reflection "in" Practice

It is not unusual for clients to dismiss changes they have made as accidental, minimal, or the result of something outside of themselves. I want Niki to take ownership for her change. It is a strength that we can use.

Dr. Z: For your mom? It seems like doing things for your mom is important, but this morning when you woke up, how did you actually motivate yourself to do all the things you needed to do in order to get to school? I know you were doing it for your mom ... but *you* are the one who did it!

Niki: I cried all morning and I worried about all my friends asking me, "How are you doing?" or simply just seeing them and thinking about the viewing and funeral and breaking down. It was horrible.

Dr. Z: Again, I'm amazed. With the image in your mind of all your friends looking and feeling sad for you, and maybe asking you how you are—over and over—and maybe even breaking down and crying, you still were able to get dressed and come to school. That's quite a strength you have and a gift to your mom!

Niki: Well, I just kept saying to myself, stop it, this will help mom feel like I'm okay, and she needs me to be strong.

Dr. Z: So, believing that being strong and going to school would help your mom was what it took for you to keep going?

Niki: Yeah.

Reflection "in" Practice

It is clear that Niki values her mom and wants to support and help her, even when doing so is uncomfortable for Niki. I want to refocus her on how this strategy worked for her.

Dr. Z: Niki, I can see how much you want to help your mom at this very difficult time. Reminding yourself that going to school would help her actually got you through all those fears that you had about friends, and breaking down. That's quite a strength.

Niki: I guess.

Dr. Z: I am wondering. I know when you woke up and thought of how the day may go, it was upsetting, but how were you feeling when you reminded yourself that this was something your mom wanted and it was something you could do to help her?

Niki: I felt like I could do something for her. She's really hurting and I wanted to help.

Dr. Z: And how did believing you could help and were helping make you feel?

Niki: I guess a little less sad, maybe hopeful that we could get through this.

Dr. Z: That's fantastic, but how does your going to school help you and your mom get through this?

Niki: She wants me to be okay. I guess she thought that if I could go to school that I was starting to be okay.

(Continued)

(Continued)

Dr. Z: Okay, so she's feeling like you were on the road back to being okay. How about you? How does coming to school help you?

Niki: I don't know. I almost feel guilty being here. Like how can I possibly have fun and hang out . . . my dad and brother are dead.

Reflection "in" Practice

It is not unusual for a client to feel ambivalent about the construction of change. I need to help Niki reframe this situation and assimilate all of these feelings.

Dr. Z: I think I can understand how you may feel guilty about getting on with your life, especially if you are moving on as if nothing has changed. But Niki, you haven't forgotten anything. Clearly, you miss your dad and your brother and are very concerned about your mom. You are so concerned about your mom that you are pushing yourself to do things that you feel will help her heal. I wonder, should she feel guilty about healing and feeling better?

Niki: No. Absolutely not!

Dr. Z: Of course not. And what do you think she would say about you feeling guilty about doing things that help you heal and feel better?

Niki: She already did. She told me that Dad and Thomas would be annoyed if we didn't get on with our lives.

Dr. Z: That's good. But, we both know getting on with your life is not easy and maybe we need to just take small steps in that direction.

Reflection "in" Practice

I was hoping to get Niki to goal consideration and perhaps goal shaping.

Niki: I guess.

Dr. Z: Okay. So you were saying that when your mom sees signs of you doing the things you used to do, like going to school, she would believe that you were beginning to handle this pretty well and were becoming somewhat okay?

Niki: Yeah. She said it's okay to be sad or angry or really upset, but she also keeps saying that I still have a lot to offer and Dad would want me to keep going.

Dr. Z: Your mom sounds like an amazing woman . . . and you apparently have many of those same qualities.

Reflection "in" Practice

Goal Setting

Now that Niki has introduced her desire to help her mom, and mom is looking for signs that Niki is moving back to a "preloss" style, maybe I can get Niki to identify an initial goal that would help her toward moving back to a life as a senior in high school.

Dr. Z: Niki, the fact that you were able to get yourself to school today was certainly a step in a good direction, according to your mom's view. How about from your perspective? How does coming to school serve you?

Niki: I guess it distracts me, although not completely.

Dr. Z: Could you tell me what that means, "distracts you"?

Niki: Well, when I was at home, I just kept thinking about the accident and my dad and brother. I was just sitting in my room crying. So, I guess coming here makes me think of other things.

Dr. Z: And thinking of other things, does that help?

Niki: Well, I am not crying and feeling sick to my stomach, like I was yesterday. So I guess it helps a little.

Reflection "in" Practice

While we may have a terminal goal in mind, I want Niki to value the fact that incremental changes, small steps toward our ultimate goal, are something to value and work toward.

Dr. Z: I guess even if it just helps a little, that's a good thing?

Niki: I guess.

Dr. Z: So, the fact that you are in school today helps your mom, a little, because she sees that you are doing the things that you did before the accident and being the way you were, again at least a little, like you were before all of this happened?

Niki: That's what she said. She said she wants me to just be a normal high school senior.

Dr. Z: And, if I understand what you said, being at school helps a little to move you away from all the thoughts and images and feelings that you had staying in your room and allows you to feel, a tiny bit, like you did before all this happened.

(Continued)

(Continued)

Niki: I guess—a little.

Dr. Z: I am wondering, if in fact you were starting to feel and act a little more like you were prior to the accident, you know, being that normal high school senior, what things other than coming to school would you or your mom notice about you?

Reflection "in" Practice

I was hoping to have Niki begin to identify a "preferred" future state. While I could have employed a miracle question, my thoughts were that Niki had provided me a focal point, that is, acting like a normal senior in high school, and it would be more useful at this state of counseling to work with her framework to set goals.

Niki: I don't know. Maybe I would not be crying all the time and I wouldn't be moping around.

Reflection "in" Practice

I need to reframe her presentation to reflect a "positive" goal.

Dr. Z: So, if you weren't moping and crying, what would you be doing instead?

Niki: Well, I have tons of stuff to do for college applications so I guess I would be working on those things and maybe being active with the prom committee, things like that.

Dr. Z: That's fantastic. But if you were doing college applications or prom work . . . what would your mom see that would suggest to her that you were beginning to return to living your life as a senior?

Niki: I don't know. Maybe I would be smiling or maybe I would have to be out and working with my friends around the prom stuff. I think if she saw me with my friends she would think that was good.

Reflection "in" Practice

Perhaps this is a point where we could explore tasks. In providing the "message," I want to be sure to provide Niki with encouragement and feedback in regards to what she has already accomplished. The compliment needs to be genuine. I will also need to summarize the strategies that she has already begun to use and try to build on those.

Dr. Z: Great, Niki. You know the fact that you came to school today is one way of showing your mom that you are trying to reengage with your friends.

Niki: Yeah, but it is hard.

Dr. Z: It is hard, but you have been able to push through that difficulty and you should feel proud of that strength. I know supporting your mom is very important to you and it is clear that you are willing to do hard work to help her, and I hope, yourself.

Niki: I guess.

Reflection "in" Practice

Setting the task for this first session, I will try to get her to be aware of things that are happening, that she would like to see continue.

Dr. Z: You said that if your mom saw you engaged with your friends, that she would see this as evidence that you are moving forward.

Niki: Yes. I said that she hopes I can get involved with school and friends again.

Dr. Z: Okay, great. So trying to interact with your friends and maybe working on school projects, or maybe prom planning, would be the kinds of things that she would like to see, and I assume you would like to do?

Niki: I do like it . . . but it still doesn't feel like before.

Dr. Z: It may take some time for you to completely get back into the flow of things, but these activities do seem to help a little. I am wondering, what other things might your mom look for that would tell her that you are doing better?

Niki: I am not sure what you mean?

Dr. Z: Well, you said you thought your mom felt better seeing you come back to school today, because she saw that as a step to getting back to doing more "normal" things.

Niki: Yeah.

Dr. Z: So, what else would your mom look for that you would be doing that would tell her that you are moving in that direction of acting and being like before?

Niki: Oh, you mean like normally I would come home and get online with my friends, or have someone come over to do homework or even may be go out for a little while.

Dr. Z: Perfect! That's exactly what I was thinking.

Niki: I'm not sure I want to do this stuff, really, who cares?

(Continued)

(Continued)

Reflection "in" Practice

Focusing on Small Steps

Niki's grief is clearly depleting her energy. She may be feeling guilt about moving back into her life or simply just doesn't have the energy required of such engagement. I need to invite her to provide a possible target of small change.

Dr. Z: Niki, let's imagine how your mom may greet you when you return from school today. What do you think she will be hoping to see or hear?

Niki: I guess she would like me to tell her I had a good day and maybe see me as less sad—a little happier?

Dr. Z: So, she would hope to see something that indicated your day was a little better and that it helped to give you some relief from the grief and sadness?

Niki: Yes.

Dr. Z: So, I'm wondering what type of things might she be looking for that you could do to tell her that coming to school today was a good thing?

Niki: You mean if I went home and told her about my day?

Dr. Z: That sounds right. Is that something you would have typically done?

Niki: Oh, yeah . . . she loves hearing about the stuff that goes on. We usually talk about stuff while we are making dinner.

Dr. Z: So how about this? I would like you to share with your mom about something that happened today at school and simply observe what happens. Maybe we could look at this and other things that may happen between now and tomorrow when we meet.

Niki: Could I tell her about meeting with you? I mean I still feel like crap, but just talking with you has helped me to be less worried.

Dr. Z: Well, that's a good thing?

Niki: And talking about the prom committee got me a little excited, but I don't think I can start working on that now.

Dr. Z: Maybe small steps are all we need, all your mother is looking for? So, do you think you could tell your mom about our meeting today and how it helped you worry less and even start to think about things like the prom that you want to eventually start doing again . . . when you are ready.

Niki: Actually, I think she would feel relieved that I spoke with you . . . especially if I can keep coming (smiling).

Dr. Z: Not only can you keep coming ... but it's a command (smiling). Seriously, maybe you could share with your mom about our meeting and then tomorrow you and I can review what you did and the impact it had on your mom, and on you, and then we can go from there? What do you think?

Niki: Thanks (tearing up). Thank you for being here. I will try, I promise.

Dr. Z: No promises necessary, just small steps (smiling).

Reflection "on" Practice

(Following the Session in Preparation for the Next Encounter)

Wow, what a courageous kid. I can't imagine the pain and turmoil she must be experiencing. I am so thankful that she has a supportive mom and that she herself has good supportive friends and is able to be self-motivated. I know she wants to do everything she can to help her mom and I need to keep her focused on helping herself and how that may look.

Next session, I need to follow-up on our mini-experiment and if it is doable, ask her a miracle question to begin to more concretely identify her goals and how we can shape these. I have to remember ... it is not a problem; it is a person. I need to let Niki set the pace since only she knows what she has to overcome and what strengths she brings to the process. This is really a time when I need to focus on "relating" before "resolving."

For the next session I will focus on:

a. providing encouragement for her efforts to work collaboratively

b. providing evidence of the possibility of change (even from last session)

c. moving to goal clarification and scaling, starting with the miracle question

d. beginning highlighting exceptions

CASE 2: CHARLES

From Complainant to Customer

Reflection "in" Practice

As I read the note from the eighth-grade teacher, I hypothesized that both Charles and Mrs. Eliason (the referring teacher) were clearly at a stalemate and apparently have been "butting heads" for some time. As I read the brief referral, it seemed to me that Mrs. Eliason was very annoyed. I was anticipating that Charles may be quite defensive.

(Continued)

(Continued)

> *This is the first time I have worked Charles and I want to be sure to set the stage for a supportive, cooperative working relationship. My goals involve inviting Charles to become a customer and for us together to focus on the positive, the goals, and avoid getting mired in problem analyses.*

Ms. G: Good morning, Charles. Come on in and take a seat. I'm Ms. Gladstone, your counselor, and I am really happy you came down to see me.

Charles: I had to come. Mrs. Eliason sent me.

Ms. G: Well, maybe Mrs. Eliason referred you, but you did come down and I am glad you did.

Charles: Whatever.

Reflection "in" Practice

My initial feelings were that Charles was really defensive and probably angry, perhaps even embarrassed. Since this was the first time he had come to the counseling office, he probably was unsure of what I was going to do. I wanted him to give direction to the session and be able to experience the support I wanted to offer.

Ms. G: Maybe it would help if you told me what happened?

Charles: It's Mrs. Eliason. She's got it out for me.

Ms. G: Got it out for you?

Charles: Yeah, she's always on me. She is always trying to make me look stupid in class. I really don't like her.

Ms. G: It sounds like things are not very positive right now. Would you help me to understand it a little better? Maybe you could tell me what happened today?

Charles: Well, we just started class and everybody was talking. I mean everybody. The whole class was clowning around. Well, she freaked out. And started telling me to "Shut up, or get out!" That really pissed me off. Sorry.

Ms. G: So, there were a lot of students talking before class, and then Mrs. Eliason was getting upset and told you to stop or get out?

Charles: She's always getting on my case. She's the one that needs help! If she'd stop picking on me, things would be good.

Reflection "in" Practice

It is clear that Charles is approaching our work as "complainant." He certainly is willing to talk about the problem, but wants to place the solution on Mrs. Eliason. I need to help him see some value in taking ownership over the solution.

Ms. G: So, it sounds like today things weren't good?

Charles: I was fine until she started.

Ms. G: So, you were fine prior to going into Mrs. Eliason's class, and even fine until class started?

Charles: Yeah.

Ms. G: Charles, what were you doing that made it fine for you?

Charles: What do you mean?

Ms. G: Well, if I understood what you were saying, it seems that you were having a good day and then you went to English class and were still having a good day, and then something happened to make it not such a great day. I am just wondering, what were you doing, or how were you acting that made it a good day?

Charles: You mean like I was clowning around with friends and that's fun?

Ms. G: Perfect. So, being with your friends and talking and clowning around, as you say, really makes the day pretty good?

Charles: Sure.

Ms. G: But if I understood, you said it was good in your other classes? I assume you weren't clowning around all through math class, were you?

Charles: Are you kidding? I have Mr. Gambone—no way!

Ms. G: Okay. But you said it was good in that class. So what do you in that class to make it good?

Charles: I like Mr. Gambone. He's tough but funny . . . and a good teacher.

Reflection "in" Practice

Charles is still externalizing the solution. I want to help him focus on what he contributes to the solution.

(Continued)

(Continued)

Ms. G: It sounds like you enjoy Mr. Gambone's class. But, I am still trying to figure out what it is you do, or how you act, that helps make Mr. Gambone's class a good one?

Charles: Well, I like math and I'm good at it, so I like to answer questions and volunteer to go the board to do problems.

Ms. G: Fantastic! That's what I was looking for. So, you really are participating in Mr. Gambone's class. You know, raising your hand and answering questions or going to the board to do problems ... fantastic!

Charles: I guess.

Ms. G: Well, what I mean is that it seems like when you are active and participating, it contributes to making that class a good one?

Charles: Hmm.

Ms. G: Like, are there any other classes that you are active in, and you know, answer questions or participate in some way?

Charles: I guess science and sometimes social studies.

Ms. G: So, if my "hypothesis" is correct, I would predict you like science and sometimes social studies (smiling).

Charles: Yeah (smiling).

Ms. G: So, it seems you have this miracle answer to making school enjoyable (smiling).

Charles: Yeah ... real superpowers!

Ms. G: I like that, "Charles the Superparticipant."

Reflection "in" Practice

Charles is clearly relaxed and able to see the positives that he brings to a couple of his other classes. I wonder if he would see this as a preferred, desirable goal for English class.

Ms. G: Charles, let me ask you to do something that I have found really helpful for myself and for some of the others students I talk with. I would like you to imagine that tonight when you go home and go to sleep, that while you are sleeping, a miracle happens. Now, you don't know that this miracle is happening, but when you wake, you start seeing signs that the miracle happened and that your school days, from this point, would all be good ones.

Charles: Oh, yeah ... it would take miracle (smiling).

Ms. G: Well, let's imagine that this miracle did happen. What would be some of the things you would see or experience that would tell you that the miracle happened?

Charles: Hmm...well, I would start at point guard (smiling).

Ms. G: Okay, anything else?

Charles: Yeah. I would have As in all my classes.

Ms. G: Sound great. Anything else?

Charles: Yeah. Mrs. E would have retired (smiling).

Reflection "in" Practice

Charles was doing well but has returned to externalizing the solution; I need him to return his focus to him.

Ms. G: Okay, I got the starting basketball thing and the As, but how would Mrs. E. retiring be evidence that a miracle happened?

Charles: I wouldn't be hassled in English class and I wouldn't be in trouble.

Ms. G: Oh, okay. So, what makes it a good day is that you wouldn't be in trouble or "hassled" in English class. Got it. But, I am wondering, what would you be doing instead?

Charles: Huh?

Ms. G: Well, if you weren't in trouble, what would you be doing?

Charles: I guess just listening, and, hmm, I don't know, participating?

Ms. G: Cool. So, if a miracle happened, you would be participating in English class just like you do in math and science, and sometimes social studies, and that would make it a really good day.

Charles: Yeah, I guess.

Ms. G: That's fantastic.

Reflection "in" Practice

I wonder if I can get Charles to embrace the role of customer? Let me see if he's able and ready to embrace a goal and even scale it.

Ms. G.   I have an idea. Since you are apparently "Mr. Science" (smiling), see this line (pointing to line on paper); at one end, I'm going place the number 10 and that represents the miracle day ... you know, you are getting

(Continued)

(Continued)

	As and participating in class and enjoying your day. And then over here, I'll put a 1, which is the worst day you could ever imagine in school in terms of grades and lack of participation . . . okay? Where would you put yourself on this scale?
Charles:	I don't know. Maybe a 6?
Ms. G:	A 6—wow! What makes it a 6?
Charles:	Well, I am getting honors and most of my classes I have A's, B+ in social studies and a B in English . . . and I like to debate in social studies class and do experiments . . . so I guess a 6.
Ms. G:	Fantastic. I wonder what a 7 or 8 would look like?
Charles:	Hmm. Maybe if I could get my English grade up to a B+ or my social studies grade to an A– that would make it better.
Ms. G:	That certainly sounds right. Would I notice anything else about you when were at 7 or 8 that I might not have seen at a 5 or 6?
Charles:	I guess you would see me being more active in class? And maybe . . . I don't know, happier?

Reflection "in" Practice

I think Charles is starting to envision a preferred future. I wonder if he's ready to investigate steps he could take to move up that scale? Maybe I can review his strengths and create a task for him to consider?

Ms. G:	Charles, that sounds really good. I am impressed that you are able to be at a 6. The fact that you are participating in some of your classes and getting some pretty good grades is super. Would moving up the scale be something that you would feel was worthwhile?
Charles:	I am not sure what you mean.
Ms. G:	I mean, would you like to be at 7 or an 8?
Charles:	I guess.
Ms. G:	Okay. Well, how about this. It appears that when you participate in class and volunteer answers in a class, that class and at least that part of the day seem to be good ones? So, what I would like you to do . . . again . . . like "Mr. Scientist," is tomorrow when you are in English class, I would like you to try to participate. Raise your hand and volunteer an answer, or get involved in the seatwork that you are doing. That kind of thing, okay?
Charles:	I don't know. I really don't like English class.

Ms. G: Well, if you tried this little experiment—you know, acting in English class like you do in science class—we would able to see if that helps make English class a little more enjoyable.

Charles: I got the idea ... but I don't know ...

Reflection "in" Practice

I need Charles to be more active in shaping the task.

Ms. G: Okay. I think it's great that you get the concept. So, how can we test our theory about the more you participate, the better the day goes?

Charles: Maybe I could start in social studies class since sometimes I just fade out there.

Ms. G: Fantastic. So, let's see. Tomorrow you will be active in social studies class. You know, asking and answering questions, if you are doing group to be a real contributor.

Charles: I can do that ... tomorrow we are discussing the elections so I can go online tonight and get information for tomorrow.

Ms. G: That's super! And, how about if we get together tomorrow before your basketball practice and we can check out the results of our "experiment"?

Charles: Okay ... but maybe you could help me become the starting point guard (laughing).

Ms. G: I'll need to work on that one (smiling).

Reflection "on" Practice

I feel good about the session. Charles is really a bright, self-motivated student and I think he left the session being a customer. He does want to do better and has very realistic goals, given his ability. I think once he sees the "evidence" of how participating in class not only leads to better grades, but also a more enjoyable day, he will be more open to consider strategies for applying this strength to his English class.

When we get together tomorrow, I want to review his "experiment," and find out in more detail how he was able to do this and maybe find an exception where he participated somewhat in English class as way of showing him it is possible. Hopefully, with that as a perspective, we will develop a plan for English class.

CASE 3: ELI

Putting Things Together

The end of this chapter provides a look a school counselor's interactions and reflections on his work with a third-grade student, Eli, who has been struggling with separation anxiety. As you review the case verbatim, you will see solution-focused concepts in action. The reflections offered prior to each section of transcript were provided by the counselor as he reflected "in" and "on" practice. It may be useful to attempt to anticipate the reflections, as well as the decisions, the counselor makes as a result of the reflections and the processing of the student's data through the lens of a solution-focused school counselor.

Reflection "on" Practice

The principal met with Mr. Benson (the counselor) and provided him the following information about Eli. Eli's parents have been divorced for about one year and the primary caregiver is Eli's mother. Recently, Eli has been staying with her father because Eli's mom has been undergoing medical treatment for breast cancer and is often weak and nauseous following chemotherapy.

With these data as context, the counselor hypothesized that Eli would be very concerned about her mom and perhaps feeling anxious and/or guilty about not being there to "help" her mom. While this was hypothesized, the counselor was also open to be surprised by the data presented by Eli.

As the counselor planned to meet with Eli, he set his target goals for the session:

1. The development of a collaborative relationship and one supportive of change.

2. Facilitation of Eli's identification of specific goals.

3. Initial identification, support, and affirmation of Eli's strengths and resources that would be useful for goal attainment.

4. Exploration of initial tasks.

As you read through the initial exchange, attempt to anticipate when and how the counselor may employ the following "strategies": empathy, accurate reflection, identification of progress made, miracle questioning, competence seeking, and exception identification. Also, take note of how each of these "strategies" contributes to the progression of the intake session and the achievement of the counselor's target goals.

Mr. B: Hi Eli. Thanks for coming down. It's really nice to see you.

Eli: Hi.

Mr. B: I know this is the first time you and I have gotten together, so I want to let you know a little about what I do. Is that okay?

Eli: Jamie Henderson talks to you and she told me you are nice.

Mr. B: Well, that's interesting. But one of thing I was going to tell you is that when I talk with someone, I won't tell other students about their coming to my office. I think that is a private kind of thing. But, you could tell people if you wanted. I may tell your mom or dad or teachers if I think that they could help in some way. Is that okay?

Eli: Yes, that's okay (starting to tear up).

Mr. B: Eli, you appear sad. Is it when I mentioned that I may talk with your mom or dad that that made you feel sad?

Eli: My mom is sick and I'm worried about her.

Mr. B: I can see you are worried. She is sick?

Eli: My mom has breast cancer. She told me. But she says that she will fine and I don't need to worry.

Mr. B: So, you and your mom are able to talk about these types of things; that sounds like you really have a good relationship with your mom. That's super!

Eli: Yeah, we talk all the time but now she's sick sometimes and just needs to rest (tearing).

Mr. B: And when she is feeling sick, you feel very sad?

Eli: I want to help but I can't.

Mr. B: You want to help?

Eli: I wish I could make her well or help her, but because she has to go to the doctors and then needs to rest she wants me to stay with my dad after school.

Mr. B: So, Eli, you want to help? That's great. And it seems like you really are helping.

Eli: How?

Mr. B: Well, it sounds like you are helping your mom by the fact that you go to your dad's after school. She needs to rest and she needs to know you are being taken care of, so that she doesn't have to worry about you. So you are helping your mom "not to worry" by going to your dad's.

Eli: I guess?

Mr. B: I assume your mom may want to go to her room and rest after her treatment.

Eli: Yeah, that's what she needs to do.

Mr. B: Okay, and I bet your mom is the kind of person who would feel bad that you were in the house, by yourself, and she couldn't talk with you or watch TV with you, or even just be around you.

(Continued)

(Continued)

Eli: That is what she said.

Mr. B: So, the fact that you go to your dad's seems to help her relax and not feel bad about you being alone. So, that's what I meant about helping her. You really do help.

Reflection "in" Practice

I feel like I am entering her world and recognize her need to do something to help her mom. It is wonderful that they have such good communication and maybe helping her see that she is already helping could open up other ways that she can feel like she is contributing to her mom's recovery. I think we are developing a good working relationship, and I think that we are setting the stage for her to see that change is possible and is, in fact, occurring.

Eli: Yeah, I understand, but I really would like to be able to do more.

Mr. B: Well, being a helper to your mom is really a good goal and we know you are already doing that by going to your dad's after school. But I have an idea. Let's imagine that tonight you go home and go to sleep and when you are asleep, a miracle happens. Now I know that the miracle you may want to happen is for your mom to be completely well and things to be back to how they were before she got sick.

Eli: I wish that could happen.

Mr. B: Me too, Eli, and it sounds like your mom's doctors are helping with that. But let's imagine that the miracle that happens is one that results in you no longer being worried about your mom and feeling like you are being the kind of helper you wish you could be, okay? So when you wake up, what would you notice that would tell you that a miracle happened and that now you are not so worried about your mom and feel like you are a bigger helper?

Eli: I guess, hmm. I guess my stomach wouldn't be feeling like I was sick or I would see my mom with energy and smiling and joking in the morning like she used to do.

Mr. B: Eli, how would seeing your mom like this be evidence that you were not so worried and were a big helper?

Eli: Well, if I saw her smiling, I would know she's okay and then I wouldn't worry.

Mr. B: Oh, okay! That's great. So, it is like, if you had some sign that your mom was okay, then you could relax?

Eli: Yeah.

Mr. B: I got that. How about the helper part? What would you notice that said you were being a helper?

Eli: I would be able to bring my mom breakfast or help her with the house or get her medicine.

Mr. B: Fantastic. And, if you were doing these things, what would your mom be doing?

Eli: She would be happier and she would tell me I was really helping.

Mr. B: Wow, that's a super miracle. So, if the miracle happened you would have lots of evidence that your mom was doing better...like she would be smiling and joking, those kinds of things, and you would be able to help her with the house chores, or getting her something to eat. Is that right?

Eli: That's what I want to do!

Mr. B: And, if you saw these things happening, you wouldn't feel so worried?

Eli: No. I would be okay, not worried.

Mr. B: And Eli, if I saw you after this miracle, what would I notice was different about you?

Eli: I guess I wouldn't be crying and daydreaming in class.

Mr. B: Okay, but I wonder what would you be doing instead of crying or daydreaming?

Eli: I think I would just be happy and talking with my friends and paying attention in class, that kind of stuff.

Mr. B: That's fantastic!

Reflection "in" Practice

Eli is very bright and insightful. I wonder if we could scale this "being happy" and find a strategy that she could use as her task for the next day or two.

Mr. B: Eli, look here (pointing to a line on his paper). If over here I placed the number 10 and I said that it stood for a time when you are really happy, and playing with your friends and really participating in class—not even the tiniest bit worried about your mom—that would be 10 on my scale. Okay? And over here, I will put a 1 and that will be the worst of all times when you are really, really sad and worried and not playing with any of your friends or not paying attention in class. Okay? Where would you say you are on this scale today?

Eli: I don't know, maybe...a 4?

(Continued)

(Continued)

Mr. B: A 4! Okay, that's good. What is it that makes you think it's a 4 today?

Eli: Well, I wasn't crying in class.

Mr. B: Okay, what were you doing in class?

Eli: Well, I was kind of quiet but I was paying attention.

Mr. B: Great. So, you were paying attention in class today. Anything else that you did that you think helped make it a 4?

Eli: Well, I guess I sat at lunch with Jamie and we talked about Hannah Montana.

Mr. B: Oh boy (smiling), another Hannah Montana fan!

Eli: Yeah (smiling).

Mr. B: So, today is a 4, meaning that you talked with a friend about something you liked, Hannah M., and you even paid attention in class. That's fantastic! But, I'm wondering, how did you do that?

Eli: I don't know.

Mr. B: Well, I mean today is pretty much like yesterday, and your mom is still getting treatment and you will still go to your dad's after school, but here you are eating lunch with Jamie and paying attention in class . . . being at 4. That's great, but how were you able to do this today?

Eli: Well, Ms. Clausen let me call my mom this morning during homeroom.

Mr. B: And that helped you be at a 4?

Eli: Well, I was able to tell her I loved her and she told me to have fun today so that she wouldn't worry about me.

Mr. B: Wow! So, you were talking with Jamie and paying attention as a way of helping your mom not to worry about you! That's fantastic helping!

Eli: Yeah, I guess.

Reflection "on" Practice

Maybe a good task for Eli, one that would serve to motivate her to be engaged in class and with her friends, might be to build on this "helping" her mom by having fun?

Mr. B: How do you think your mom would feel if you told her about you and Jamie talking about Hannah Montana during lunch?

Eli: She knows that's all we talk about.

Mr. B: I bet. But how do you think she would feel knowing that's how you spent your lunch period?

Eli: I think she would be happy 'cause she would know that I was having fun.

Mr. B: Fantastic. So I'm wondering, do you think that if you shared that with her that you would be helping her to feel better?

Eli: Yeah, I know she would like that.

Mr. B: Great. So, I have an idea. First of all, I hope you tell her all the details about the Hannah Montana discussion (smiling). But I'm wondering if between now and when I see you tomorrow, I wonder if you would think of other things that you could do in school that your mom would really enjoy hearing about and would be your way of helping.

Eli: You mean like paying attention in class.

Mr. B: Absolutely. That's great. But maybe there's even more. You just need to think about it as you go through the day. Would you do that?

Eli: Sure. I bet she would like hearing about the cheer squad meeting that we had.

Mr. B: See, you are on a roll . . . and that's a good helper.

Reflection "on" Practice

After Eli left, I thought about her and the reality that as a fourth grader, she certainly is getting a lesson on life that thankfully many fourth graders don't have to experience. But even with that, it's amazing how insightful she is. She really wants to help and is very clear about how she would be if things were fine with her mom. I think we identified a really useful task for her and I will call her down tomorrow to see, first, if she told her mom about the day and if it did have the positive impact we thought it would. But I also think that I will have her identify other strategies for being happy and sharing that with her mom.

I am really hoping to review the task performance and consolidate the changes she made (i.e., going home and sharing the positives in her day). It might be worthwhile to revisit the miracle question and help her to continue to reframe it so that she in fact can experience small changes toward her goal.

The counselor in this situation saw Eli the next day, and together they reinforced the "strategy" of engaging in school and then reporting these positive experiences back to her mom at the end of the day. This strategy helped Eli to feel

(Continued)

(Continued)

that she was helping her mom feel better, a point highlighted by the counselor, and it served the purpose of focusing Eli on things that made her relaxed and productive in school.

The counselor saw Eli three more times over the span of two weeks. During their last session, Eli informed the counselor that her mom was still in treatment, but had more energy and was more like herself, and she and her mom were back to their routine of talking in the morning at breakfast. Eli described herself as being "really involved" in school and the cheer squad, and as result, the "formal" contract was ended.

A CAVEAT

Hopefully, the case illustrations presented within this chapter provided you with the flavor of the reflections of a school counselor employing a solution-focused frame of reference. Clearly, the cases employed were those where success was evident. This was done for both ease of demonstration and in response to the reality of page limitation.

Cases do not always go as smoothly as suggested. Often the client returns to externalization of the problem or perhaps resists becoming a customer. The solution-focused school counselor continues to employ skills of effective communication and relationship building to identify the student's goals, amplify strengths and successes, and highlight the reality that change is not only possible but has in fact occurred. Throughout the work with a student, the counselor may find the need to revisit the goals by way of the miracle question, rescale the goals, and attempt to shed a different light—a different perspective—on the problem so that the student constructs goals and solutions rather than continue to be mired in problems and limitations.

WHAT'S NEXT?

In the final chapter, you will once again be provided with case illustrations. However, this time, in addition to observing a school counselor operating with a solution-focused frame of reference, you will be invited to participate. At various points in the case presentation, you will be asked to reflect on what is happening and what it is that you would do next in the process. The hope is that by stepping into the dialogue you will be able to translate your understanding of the solution-focused model into its application.

Practice in Procedural Thinking

7

The previous chapter presented examples of solution-focused counselors as they reflected "in" and "on" their practice. The cases illustrated the counselors' procedural thinking as they responded to the material and information provided by their students. The current chapter invites you to move beyond simply observing solution-focused procedural thinking to engaging in that very process.

This final chapter provides two case studies for review and guided practice. As you read the case material, you will note places where the counselor is reflecting "in" or "on" practice and is using that reflection to guide his or her actions. However, prior to viewing the counselor's reflection and decision, you will be invited to use the solution-focused lens to anticipate the counselor's response. It is hoped that with this type of practice, you will move from understanding the theory of solution-focused counseling, to employing the solution-focused framework to guide your own reflection "in" and "on" practice.

One final note is necessary prior to presenting the cases. The cases presented within this chapter may also be found in the companion texts within this series. The reason for this replication is that it will provide readers the opportunity to compare and contrast the variations in reflections and practice of school counselors operating with varied orienting frameworks.

RANDALL: THE SIXTH-GRADE BULLY

History and Context

Tammy Schulman is the middle school counselor at E. L. Richardson Middle School. Ms. Schulman receives a referral from the assistant principal that reads:

> *Tammy, I've been hearing numerous complaints from teachers and students about Randall Jenkins. While we are only three weeks into the school year, Randall has already accrued ten demerits for fighting. It is clear that unless we do something, Randall won't be here by midterm. Please see him as soon possible.*

Prior to seeing Randall, Ms. Schulman reviews his cumulative folder. Ms. Schulman discovers very little information in the folder, other than that Randall is a recent transfer to E. L. Richardson. His previous school had yet to send relevant files. However, what Ms. Schulman does discover is that Randall is new to the district, after moving here with his mother following his parents' divorce. As Ms. Schulman sits waiting for Randall to come down in response to her request to see him, she reflects on what she hopes to accomplish as a result of this initial meeting.

Reflection "in" Practice

If you were the solution-focused counselor about to meet Randall, what goals might you have for this initial session and how might you go about achieving these?

As she sits at her desk, Ms. Schulman jots down a couple of reminders: "collaboration," "empathy," "customer," "goal," "encouragement." It is clear from her notes that she anticipates that Randall may enter counseling unsure of the need or value of the counseling and may in fact be defensive and in need of support. While hoping to identify Randall's goals, Ms. Schulman clearly values the need to engage Randall as a "customer."

Ms. S: Randall, come in. Thanks for coming. I'm Ms. Schulman, the sixth-grade counselor.

Randall: (Looks down, and sits without talking.)

Ms. S: Randall, do you know why I asked to see you?

Randall: (Still looks down, and shows little response.)

Ms. S: Randall, you look a little uncomfortable, are you mad at me for some reason?

Randall: (Looks up, somewhat surprised by the question.)

Ms. S: Thanks for looking up. I wasn't sure if I was doing something wrong, because you look really unhappy. Are you unhappy right now?

Randall: (Nods yes, still not talking.)

Reflections "in" Practice

As a solution-focused counselor working with Randall, what do you feel is your immediate goal and how might you get there?

Looking at Randall, Ms. Schulman "feels" as if he is building a self-protected buttress—arms crossed, chin on his chest, looking down, and showing minimal responses. Her read is that he is preparing for an assault and clearly being defensive. With this interpretation, she feels that she needs to demonstrate support and encouragement and invite Randall to set the direction for the session.

Ms. S: Randall, I am really sorry that you are unhappy. I wish I could help, but I am really amazed that even being this unhappy, you were still able to come down here and meet with me.

Randall: I had to come—you sent for me.

Ms. S: Yes, I guess that is correct, but you did come and I appreciate that, and really appreciate you talking with me now.

Randall: Yeah, okay.

Reflection "in" Practice

Randall has opened a tiny bit. At this point, sensing his immediate problem of being "unhappy" and apparently defensive, what might your next move be?

With Randall at least now showing some minimal willingness to engage verbally, Ms. Schulman wonders if even at the very early point in the relationship, if asking the miracle question may empower Randall to set the direction—a direction that would be more positive and goal oriented.

Ms. S: Randall, I wonder if you would do something for me that some of the other students have done and have liked?

Randall: I guess.

(Continued)

(Continued)

Ms. S: That's super, thanks. Well, I'm wondering if you and I could create magic—I know we can't—but if we really could magically make things the absolute way you would want them to be, I wonder what would be some of things you would notice when you leave my office that would tell you our magic really worked?

Randall: I'd be in my old my house.

Ms. S: Okay. So, you would walk out of this office and you would be in your old house. Does that mean your old school as well?

Randall: Yeah, just like it was before.

Ms. S: Wow. That sounds like magic happened. But I am wondering, what would you notice about you? Would the magic have made you different?

Randall: I'd be with my dad and my friends (starting to tear up).

Ms. S: It seems like leaving your old neighborhood and friends and moving here, away from your dad, was really hard?

Randall: Yeah (trying to hold back tears).

Ms. S: I can see that you miss your dad and your old friends.

Reflection "in" Practice

Randall is clearly sad by the absence of his father and his relocation to this new school. As a solution-focused counselor, what would you invite Randall to focus on at this juncture?

Ms. Schulman, reflecting on the interaction, is encouraged by Randall's engagement in the dialogue but wants to direct his attention to goals and the possibility of change, rather than invite his elaboration on the problem of missing his dad and his friends.

Ms. S: So, okay. Our magic really worked and you would be with your friends from your old school, but I'm still wondering, how would that work for you? I mean, if I was observing you, what would I see that would tell me that magic happened?

Randall: I wouldn't be in any trouble and seeing a counselor.

Ms. S: So, if you weren't in trouble, what would you be doing instead?

Randall: I'd be laughing and joking with my friends.

Ms. S: In class?

Randall: Well, maybe a little, but like at lunch and in between classes, that kind of stuff.

Ms. S: Great, I think I got it. How about if I was watching in your classes? Would there be anything that I would see that would tell me magic happened?

Randall: I guess. I would be happy and participating in class, that kind of stuff.

Ms. S: Wow. That sounds super.

Randall: I wish I could go back to my old school.

Reflection "in" Practice

On first blush, it looks like Randall has a goal—to move back to his old school. How would you work with this goal?

Ms. Schulman, reflecting on Randall's goal, realizes that he will not be able to return to his old school or live with his dad, but she wonders whether returning to his old school is really the goal, or maybe a strategy toward a goal. She wonders if she can reframe the situation for Randall.

Ms. S: Randall, as I listen to you, it seems that there actually may be two goals here? I know you said one goal would be that you were back in your old school. Is that correct?

Randall: Yeah.

Ms. S: But, as you described what that looked like, it seems that maybe the other goal—maybe even the real goal—is that you would be happy and laughing and joking and having friends, and even participating in class. I wonder, if our magic made that happen, how would you feel about that?

Randall: I'd like that, but it isn't going to happen in this dumb school—everybody hates me.

Reflection "in" Practice

Randall is externalizing the problem. It's not him, it's everybody else. How might the solution-focused counselor work with this externalization?

Ms. Schulman identifies Randall's externalization and wants to go with it. Rather than placing the problem "within" Randall, and thus implying he needs to

(Continued)

(Continued)

be fixed, she wants to go with the difficulty as being outside of him and something he could work "with" and something that she could "join with him" in addressing.

Ms. S: I bet you would like it if you had friends and were laughing and joking. Maybe you could help me understand something. In your old school, was everybody always nice and friendly, or were there times when some of your friends were a bit grouchy?

Randall: Yeah, we all get like that.

Ms. S: Can you remember any one of your friends who might have gotten that way, and at least for a little while, was not so nice?

Randall: Sure. Ramone—he was grumpy a lot.

Ms. S: And when Ramone was grumpy, what would you do?

Randall: Usually just let him be . . . you know, not bug him . . . kind of just stay low.

Ms. S: Wow, that's pretty cool. Did that help Ramone, staying low?

Randall: Sometimes, and sometimes I would ask him if he wanted to shoot baskets with me or something like that.

Ms. S: Randall, you really have some super skills. I mean, here's one of your classmates who is maybe not being the nicest person this day, and you would either just stay low and just let him be, or if you thought it was a good idea, you would ask him to shoot baskets with you. Wow, that is super.

Randall: Yeah, but it didn't always work . . . sometimes he would just stay angry.

Ms. S: Okay. And if he would stay angry, what would you do?

Randall: Just leave him alone until the next day, and he usually was better.

Ms. S: Fantastic . . . that really seems smart. You have some really neat ways to cope with grouchy friends.

Reflection "in" Practice

Ms. Schulman has certainly unearthed some of Randall's strengths—and coping skills. How might you use this information to direct the remainder of this session?

Ms. Schulman is really impressed with Randall and his ability to "read" his grouchy friend and know when to leave him alone or engage with him. This is a skill that may be useful if applied to the current situation. She feels that maybe she could work this into the "task" as she moves to closing this session.

Ms. S: Randall, I really appreciate you helping today. I mean, I think I have a good idea of what it is you would hope would happen . . . you know, have friends, and be happy and even participate in class. These sound like great goals.

Randall: Yeah, but it's not like that here.

Ms. S: Well, the other thing you showed me today is some of your very special powers.

Randall: Huh?

Ms. S: Well, I mean you seem to have the ability to know when somebody is grumpy and then you even know sometimes how to invite him to play and hopefully become less grumpy.

Randall: Yeah, but that doesn't always work. Sometimes Ramone would just get angry at me and tell me to leave him alone.

Ms. S: Sure, I understand, but the cool thing is that you would leave him alone . . . you know, you would just stay low . . . 'cause you figured he would be better the next day. Isn't that right?

Randall: Yeah . . . I guess.

Ms. S: Well, that's what I meant by having special powers—you really seemed to know how to make and keep friends by inviting them to hang out and play, or when you have to, to just stay low and give them some space.

Randall: Yeah.

Ms. S: I am wondering. Have you been able to use your special powers here— you know, invite the kids to shoot baskets or skateboard or just do stuff?

Randall: No (sounding angry).

Ms. S: No?

Randall: Nobody likes me.

Reflection "in" Practice

Randall is engaging with the counselor, but as the counselor, what would you now attempt to address?

Ms. Schulman is very aware that Randall has strengths and resources that would serve him well at his new school, but at this point, he appears to be taking the posture of a complainant, rather than customer. She feels it is important for him to set his goal and believe that goal achievement is possible.

(Continued)

(Continued)

Ms. S: So, some of the kids here make it hard to play with them or hang out? Real grumps (smiling)?

Randall: Yeah, worse than Ramone . . . that's for sure (smiling), and they get me in trouble.

Ms. S: Randall, if I was watching you and your classmates during the times when you said they were getting you in trouble, what would I see you doing?

Randall: I don't know. Sometimes they get me so mad that I might say something bad.

Ms. S: So, you may get angry and say something bad?

Randall: Yeah, and then I get in trouble.

Ms. S: Okay. I think I understand that, but I'm wondering if I saw you when Ramone was grumpy, how would you be acting then?

Randall: Remember—superpowers (smiling).

Ms. S: Sorry . . . yep, so you would either just lay low or ask him to do something with you, right?

Randall: Most of the time.

Ms. S: So, with Randall, you would use your superpowers rather than saying something bad?

Randall: Yeah.

Reflection "in" Practice

The time for this school contact is brief and Ms. Schulman would like to move to exploring a task. What task might you target? And how would you present it?

Ms. Schulman is really happy that Randall has engaged and has even identified a goal and some resources he brings to that goal attainment. She wants to be sure to compliment Randall on what he has provided, and invite him to consider some of his positive strategies that he uses. Perhaps he would engage in a mini-experiment.

Ms. S: Randall, you know I really appreciate your willingness to talk with me. I am really impressed by the fact that you know what you would like to experience, like having friends, and I am amazed at your ability to make friends. You really do have good skills.

Randall: Yeah.

Ms. S: I wonder if you would be willing to do a little experiment, and then meet me tomorrow and tell me how it went?

Randall: I don't know. What do I have to do?

Ms. S: Well, you told me that when Ramone was grumpy, you would just lay low, and kind of observe and be quiet, and if you thought the time was right, you would ask him to play. Right?

Randall: Yeah.

Ms. S: Well, I am wondering what it would be like if, for the rest of today, you could do just that. You know, lay low and just listen to the other kids and try to remember what they are talking about. I don't mean every detail, but the general kinds of things they talk about. And if one of the kids is grumpy, maybe you could pretend he's Ramone and treat him like you would treat Ramone? What do you think? Could you try that for me?

Randall: I guess.

Ms. S: Well, it may be cool to see how they react to you when all you are doing is laying low?

Randall: Yeah, that would be weird, 'cause I'm always talking about my old school and they always tell me to shut up, and that's when the fights start.

Ms. S: Well, Mr. Superpowers (smiling), are you ready to lay low and treat grumpies like they are all Ramone?

Randall: Yep . . .

Ms. S: Super! And tomorrow, you and I can talk during homeroom.

Randall: Okay. Do I just come down or will you send for me?

Ms. S: I'll send for you, okay? So, let's get you back to class and your "mini-experiment," and I'll see you tomorrow. Thanks, Randall. I really do appreciate you coming down and talking with me.

Reflection "in" Practice

As Randall leaves your office and you collect your thoughts, what sticks out from the session that lays the foundation for tomorrow's meeting?

As Ms. Schulman gathers her thoughts, she is quite aware and happy that the Randall who left the office was not the same Randall who entered. She feels that she was able to join with him and to articulate an achievable goal. She was very happy to identify his coping skills and he seemed like a customer wanting to test out this "mini-experiment" and return to process the data. She feels very good about the session and the collaborative relationship established. She is more than aware that things don't always go smoothly, and hopes that tomorrow she can help Randall identify his goal in more concrete terms, and together they can goal scale and develop (and reinforce) strategies for movement up the scale.

MARIA: JUST CAN'T SAY NO!

History and Context

We pick up the case of Maria following the initial intake. Maria asked to see her school counselor, Robert Richardson, and presented her concerns about her "partying" behavior. During the first session, it was clear that Maria was a motivated "customer" who came with an agenda and a desire to work collaboratively to reach her goal.

Throughout the first session, Maria outlined her problem as "partying" too much and expressed concern that she couldn't say no to getting "high." Using the miracle question, Mr. Richardson and Maria were able to envision a preferred future with the following characteristics:

1. Maria would be very social on weekends, going out with her friends who were straight edge (no drinking or drugs).

2. Maria would be scheduling her time after school to do her schoolwork, and continue with her dance lessons.

3. Maria would be active in her gym and exercise program.

4. Maria would be more knowledgeable about health food, diets, and nutrition for professional dancers and would be consistently following that plan.

The first meeting was cut short due to a modified Friday class schedule, but Mr. Richardson was able to have Maria use the scaling technique to identify where she currently saw herself in reference to this preferred future. She placed herself at a 3, which she described as sometimes going to the gym, and trying not to eat junk food. In ending the session, Mr. Richardson summarized the 10 in her preferred future, and after reflecting her self-description as a 3, he asked Maria to consider, as concretely as possible, what it would look like if she were at a 4 or a 5. They scheduled to meet on Monday following her weekend.

Reflection "in" Practice

Assuming you are Maria's counselor, now reflecting on your first session and the "task" identified, what might you, as a solution-focused school counselor, set as your goals for this second session?

Mr. Richardson is very hopeful and optimistic that given Maria's initial motivation and insights, that she will have some concrete descriptions of a 4 or a 5. With these as reference points, he hopes that in their meeting today he will:

1. Identify any changes that occurred between sessions and consolidate these constructive changes.

2. Review the tasks.

3. Construct solutions.

4. Continue to deconstruct the problem.

Mr. R: Hi Maria. Come on in. Well Maria, could you bring me up to speed? What has changed since our meeting on Friday?

Maria: Not so good, Mr. Richardson. I left Friday really determined. I made a commitment that I was going to get serious about my dancing and getting myself healthy.

Mr. R: Maria, that is fantastic. You seemed really committed and motivated when we met, but it sounds like that even became a stronger commitment the more you thought about it?

Maria: It was . . . and I did great Friday night. I actually went and met a trainer at the gym and we set a weekly program where I would meet with him three times a week.

Mr. R: Wow, fantastic.

Maria: Yeah, but Saturday was not so fantastic. I was beat from working out Friday night and little sore (smiles). So, I was planning to just stay in and work on my social studies project. Well around 8:30—hmm—well, I get a call that there's a party and do I want to go? At first I said no. I really did. But . . . you don't need to know who it was . . . but anyway, this girl just kept working me. Things like come on it will be fun, and we'll stay just a little while . . . things like that. Anyway I caved in and went . . . and got high. Sorry.

Mr. R: Maria, this change stuff is really, really hard. It's hard work. You don't have to apologize. Look at the things you did differently. I mean, Friday you went to the gym. Saturday you started on your project. That's different. Those sounds like the type of things that would move you up our scale toward your goal?

Maria: Yeah, but I still blew it. I got high!

Mr. R: Well, Saturday wasn't a 10, but again, you did something that if I understood correctly, you didn't do before, and that is said "no."

Maria: Yeah, I guess.

Reflection "in" Practice

Mr. Richardson is doing a good job identifying small steps, changes that occurred and reinforcing them. At the same time, his reaction to her getting high is supportive, nonjudgmental, and certainly provides the climate for change to occur. But now we are at a spot where a decision needs to be made. Do we investigate the party and getting high, or is there another direction you would take if you were this solution-focused counselor?

(Continued)

(Continued)

Mr. Richardson sees a big change—Maria's willingness to say no to her friend and the party, and he not only wants to consolidate that change, but also employ learning and maintenance strategies in order to increase her resolve and her ability to say no.

Mr. R: Maria, last Friday you told me how you were going out almost every Friday and Saturday and getting high, and now here it is and you get this phone call and you actually said no. How did you do that?

Maria: I don't know. I was working on my project and actually getting into it, so that when she called and said let's go party, I just kind of thought about my project and wanted to continue so I told her no, I'm doing some stuff for school and wanted to get it done.

Mr. R: Wow. So you actually just told her that you preferred doing schoolwork to getting high?

Maria: Well, not exactly those words (smiling), but that's what she heard. She goes, "Yeah right little miss school girl" and then started cutting up and things and before you knew it, we were talking about the people who were going to be there, and then I said okay.

Mr. R: So, if you really take a look at this situation, what did you learn?

Maria: Don't answer the phone (smiling).

Mr. R: Well, I guess that's one way, but that doesn't help you say no.

Maria: I guess. When I am doing things—like when I was at the gym Friday—I wasn't even thinking about partying . . . and even Saturday when I was doing the project. So maybe if I kept busy, it would help.

Mr. R: That sounds good. But I know one of the elements to your miracle question was that you would be social on weekends?

Maria: Yeah, that's where I get into problems.

Reflection "in" Practice

Maria has identified some coping skills, like keeping busy, and while these are useful, they don't facilitate her ability to have healthy, desirable social encounters. At this point in the session, what might you do to continue the discussion of solution strategies?

Mr. Richardson has used questions geared to identifying how Maria was able to resist (i.e., learning strategies). He now wants to identify an exception where she has been social with her straight-edged friends and hopefully said no to the partying.

If he can identify this exception, he will ask questions that will help Maria identify things she needs to do to increase the use of these skills (i.e., maintenance questions).

Mr. R: Last time, you said you wanted to hang out with your "straight-edged" friends. Have you done that in the past?

Maria: Oh, yeah a lot.

Mr. R: That's great. I wonder, have you had a situation where you may have made plans to do something with these friends and then somebody invites you to a party to get high, and you said no, that you were busy?

Maria: That's what I used to do a lot. But then I started partying pretty regularly and saying no to my straight-edged friends.

Mr. R: Okay, but could you think of a time when you said no to paryting and went with your other friends?

Maria: Yeah, on my birthday—that was last month—Liz, Harold, Jamal, and Robert, these are some of the friends I call straight edged, they planned to take me out for my birthday and right before I was supposed to meet them, I got a text message and then a phone call telling me that there was a major party planned in my honor and everybody was going to get wasted.

Mr. R: Wow, two parties but you said no to the drugs and went with Liz and everybody?

Maria: Yeah. Boy, that was hard, but I didn't want to disappoint Liz and those guys.

Mr. R: That is fantastic. You really care about and value their friendship.

Maria: Yeah, they are great. They are even hanging with me this past month and I am just a jerk (getting upset). Maybe I have an addictive personality?

Reflection "in" Practice

Maria has identified an excellent exception to her partying, but she seems to be placing a lot of the power on her friends and labeling herself as a "jerk" or possibly an addictive personality. How would you intervene at this stage of the process?

While excited about the exception provided by Maria, Mr. Richardson is concerned about her self-labeling. With his constructivist orientation, he knows that labels can become experienced realities and in this situation would disempower Maria. He decides to reframe the "problem" using externalization. He feels this will put the problem out there as something that she can battle, rather than something that is inside her and hopelessly hard wired.

(Continued)

(Continued)

Mr. R: The fact that you were able to say no to getting high on your birthday is pretty fantastic. What do you think that says about you?

Maria: I don't know. I guess sometimes I can make good decisions.

Mr. R: Absolutely you have that ability. But it is hard, and the invitation to party is out there and it is really strong.

Maria: Yeah. I wish I could just say *no*.

Mr. R: And you did! You did on your birthday and you did even Saturday . . . but that invitation—that call—can be really inviting.

Maria: But when I know there is something better—you know, healthier to do—I can say no to the invitation.

Mr. R: Maria, you are really something. I love the way you said you *can* say no to the invitation. And, you do say no. And as you pointed out, you can say no when it's clear there is something better and healthier to do. So what could you do this week to identify these healthier things to do?

Maria: Well, that shouldn't be too hard. We have finals in a week so I was going to finish up my project in social studies, and then this weekend Robert and Jamal were going to study for our AP tests.

Mr. R: Wow, that's sound like a great plan.

Maria: Oh yeah . . . I have the gym three times this week and dance class Thursday night.

Mr. R: Wow! You are one active lady (smiling)!

Reflection "in" Practice

Mr. Richardson has helped to reframe the problem as a very tempting invitation, but one that Maria does not need to be victim to—rather, it is one that she can and has turned down. As we come to the end of this session, we want to turn our attention to setting a task. How might you use the scaling process and the review of this session to identify a task for Maria to enact over the course of the coming week?

Mr. Richardson is aware that the session needs to come to end and that Maria needs to get ready for her next class. He is also aware that he hasn't reviewed the previous task of having Maria identify what a 4 or 5 may look like. He decides to take the last few minutes to not only encourage Maria and compliment her for hard work and achievements, but also visit the scaling again and use that to set a task.

Mr. R: Maria, we only have a few minutes before the next class. But I have to tell you, you have done a fantastic job. I mean, the exception you were able to identify, the plans you have already put in place, these things were not easy but you have done them and that's fantastic.

Maria: Thanks. I think I can do it.

Mr. R: Well, I am confident you will do it. But let's take small steps . . . just like in dance class or the gym . . . small steps are progress.

Maria: That's for sure.

Mr. R: I know I asked you to think about how a 4 or 5 would look on our scale. Were you able to do that?

Maria: Oh, yeah. I decided that if I was at a 4, I would be eating three healthy meals and no junk food and I would be going to the gym at least once a week.

Mr. R: Wait a minute . . . but you did that! So you are already at a 4?

Maria: Yeah, but now I want to move up. I want to be able to say no and really stick with it.

Mr. R: That sounds like quite a jump. How about this. You were able to say a big no on your birthday not just because you had something else to do, but because you knew it would disappoint your good friends. Is that right?

Maria: Yeah.

Mr. R: Okay. So I know you have already made plans for this weekend to work on your project and get together for study group. But how about if you think of things you need to remember or maybe things you could do whenever that "invitation" starts to look inviting. And then next, maybe you could stop down and let me know what's happened?

Maria: I can do that. You know, I could even ask Jamal to maybe help me out. He and I have talked about stuff like this and I know he would be like my sponsor (smiling).

Mr. R: See, you are always thinking. But let's go slow. Think about it, and for now, go hit those books and the gym . . . (smiling) ouch! And I'll see you later.

Reflection "on" Practice

Assuming you were the counselor in this session, now reflecting on the session:

- *What is your evaluation of the session?*
- *Do you feel Maria is a customer?*
- *Is there a need to reconsider the goals, or do they appear achievable?*

(Continued)

(Continued)

> - *Do we need to test Maria's constructs, especially in regard to speed with which she can achieve her 10?*
> - *How about employing the aid of Jamal?*
> - *Where do you start with the next session?*

Mr. Richardson really enjoys working with Maria. He sees her as bright and self-motivated. He is a tiny bit concerned that she may be expecting too much from herself, and he is prepared to help her reframe any setbacks as opportunities to learn rather than failures.

As he thinks about the upcoming session he sets as his goals:

- Identify and consolidate any changes that have occurred during the week.
- Revisit the scale.
- Allow Maria to share her insights regarding the value of including Jamal in her solution strategies.
- Using the scale, identify with Maria a target point that would signal the termination of the regular, scheduled counseling sessions.

Mr. Richardson knows that, as her counselor, he will continue to see her—about issues of college choices, career planning, and other events in the life of a high school student, but he also wants to come to a clear understanding about when this contract will be coming to an end.

Epilogue

A Beginning . . . Not an End

While we have come to the end of this book, it is hopefully only the beginning of your own ongoing development as a reflective school counselor. The material presented in this book has provided you with an introduction to the world of a solution-focused school counselor, and the procedural thinking that guides his or her practice. However, it is truly just the beginning.

As school counselors, we know the value of maintaining competence in the skills we use and we know the ethical mandate to continue to develop those skills (See Resource, Standard E.1.c). While being open to new procedures demonstrated to be effective for the diverse population with whom we work, we must also recognize the limitations of our professional competence to use these procedures (See Resource, Standard E.1.a). The material provided in this book is but a first step to developing that competency.

Becoming an expert in counseling, as is true of any profession, requires continued training, personal reflection, and supervision. It is hoped that with this introduction to the theory and practice of a solution-focused counselor, you will be stimulated to continue in that training, personal reflection, and supervision and as a result grow in thinking and acting like an expert.

Resource

Ethical Standards for School Counselors

The American School Counselor Association's (ASCA) Ethical Standards for School Counselors were adopted by the ASCA Delegate Assembly, March 19,1984, revised March 27, 1992, June 25, 1998 and June 26, 2004. For a PDF version of the Ethical Standards visit www.schoolcounselor.org/content.asp?contentid=173.

PREAMBLE

The American School Counselor Association (ASCA) is a professional organization whose members are certified/licensed in school counseling with unique qualifications and skills to address the academic, personal/ social, and career development needs of all students. Professional school counselors are advocates, leaders, collaborators, and consultants who create opportunities for equity in access and success in educational opportunities by connecting their programs to the mission of schools and subscribing to the following tenets of professional responsibility:

- Each person has the right to be respected, be treated with dignity, and have access to a comprehensive school counseling program that advocates for and affirms all students from diverse populations regardless of ethnic/racial status, age, economic status, special needs, English as a second language or other language group, immigration status, sexual orientation, gender, gender identity/expression, family type, religious/spiritual identity, and appearance.
- Each person has the right to receive the information and support needed to move toward self-direction and self-development and affirmation

within one's group identities, with special care being given to students who have historically not received adequate educational services: students of color, low socioeconomic students, students with disabilities and students with nondominant language backgrounds.

- Each person has the right to understand the full magnitude and meaning of his or her educational choices and how those choices will affect future opportunities.
- Each person has the right to privacy and thereby the right to expect the counselor-student relationship to comply with all laws, policies, and ethical standards pertaining to confidentiality in the school setting.

In this document, ASCA specifies the principles of ethical behavior necessary to maintain the high standards of integrity, leadership, and professionalism among its members. The Ethical Standards for School Counselors were developed to clarify the nature of ethical responsibilities held in common by school counseling professionals. The purposes of this document are to:

- Serve as a guide for the ethical practices of all professional school counselors regardless of level, area, population served or membership in this professional association.
- Provide self-appraisal and peer evaluations regarding counselor responsibilities to students, parents/guardians, colleagues, and professional associates, schools, communities, and the counseling profession.
- Inform those served by the school counselor of acceptable counselor practices and expected professional behavior.

A.1. Responsibilities to Students

The professional school counselor:

a. Has a primary obligation to the student, who is to be treated with respect as a unique individual.

b. Is concerned with the educational, academic, career, personal, and social needs and encourages the maximum development of every student.

c. Respects the student's values and beliefs and does not impose the counselor's personal values.

d. Is knowledgeable of laws, regulations, and policies relating to students and strives to protect and inform students regarding their rights.

A.2. Confidentiality

The professional school counselor:

a. Informs students of the purposes, goals, techniques, and rules of procedure under which they may receive counseling at or before the time when the counseling relationship is entered. Disclosure notice includes the limits of confidentiality such as the possible necessity for consulting with other professionals, privileged communication, and legal or authoritative restraints. The meaning and limits of confidentiality are defined in developmentally appropriate terms to students.

b. Keeps information confidential unless disclosure is required to prevent clear and imminent danger to the student or others or when legal requirements demand that confidential information be revealed. Counselors will consult with appropriate professionals when in doubt as to the validity of an exception.

c. In absence of state legislation expressly forbidding disclosure, considers the ethical responsibility to provide information to an identified third party who, by his or her relationship with the student, is at a high risk of contracting a disease that is commonly known to be communicable and fatal. Disclosure requires satisfaction of all of the following conditions:

   • Student identifies partner or the partner is highly identifiable.
   • Counselor recommends the student notify partner and refrain from further high-risk behavior.
   • Student refuses.
   • Counselor informs the student of the intent to notify the partner.
   • Counselor seeks legal consultation as to the legalities of informing the partner.

d. Requests of the court that disclosure not be required when the release of confidential information may potentially harm a student or the counseling relationship.

e. Protects the confidentiality of students' records and releases personal data in accordance with prescribed laws and school policies. Student information stored and transmitted electronically is treated with the same care as traditional student records.

f. Protects the confidentiality of information received in the counseling relationship as specified by federal and state laws, written policies, and applicable ethical standards. Such information is only to be revealed to others with the informed consent of the student, consistent with the counselor's ethical obligation.

g. Recognizes his or her primary obligation for confidentiality is to the student but balances that obligation with an understanding of the legal and inherent rights of parents/guardians to be the guiding voice in their children's lives.

A.3. Counseling Plans

The professional school counselor:

a. Provides students with a comprehensive school counseling program that includes a strong emphasis on working jointly with all students to develop academic and career goals.

b. Advocates for counseling plans supporting students' right to choose from the wide array of options when they leave secondary education. Such plans will be regularly reviewed to update students regarding critical information they need to make informed decisions.

A.4. Dual Relationships

The professional school counselor:

a. Avoids dual relationships that might impair his or her objectivity and increase the risk of harm to the student (e.g., counseling one's family members, close friends, or associates). If a dual relationship is unavoidable, the counselor is responsible for taking action to eliminate or reduce the potential for harm. Such safeguards might include informed consent, consultation, supervision, and documentation.

b. Avoids dual relationships with school personnel that might infringe on the integrity of the counselor/student relationship.

A.5. Appropriate Referrals

The professional school counselor:

a. Makes referrals when necessary or appropriate to outside resources. Appropriate referrals may necessitate informing both parents/guardians and students of applicable resources and making proper plans for transitions with minimal interruption of services. Students retain the right to discontinue the counseling relationship at any time.

A.6. Group Work

The professional school counselor:

a. Screens prospective group members and maintains an awareness of participants' needs and goals in relation to the goals of the group. The counselor takes reasonable precautions to protect members from physical and psychological harm resulting from interaction within the group.

b. Notifies parents/guardians and staff of group participation if the counselor deems it appropriate and if consistent with school board policy or practice.

c. Establishes clear expectations in the group setting and clearly states that confidentiality in group counseling cannot be guaranteed. Given the developmental and chronological ages of minors in schools, the counselor recognizes the tenuous nature of confidentiality for minors renders some topics inappropriate for group work in a school setting.

d. Follows up with group members and documents proceedings as appropriate.

A.7. Danger to Self or Others

The professional school counselor:

a. Informs parents/guardians or appropriate authorities when the student's condition indicates a clear and imminent danger to the student or others. This is to be done after careful deliberation and, where possible, after consultation with other counseling professionals.

b. Will attempt to minimize threat to a student and may choose to (1) inform the student of actions to be taken, (2) involve the student in a three-way communication with parents/guardians when breaching confidentiality, or (3) allow the student to have input as to how and to whom the breach will be made.

A.8. Student Records

The professional school counselor:

a. Maintains and secures records necessary for rendering professional services to the student as required by laws, regulations, institutional procedures, and confidentiality guidelines.

b. Keeps sole-possession records separate from students' educational records in keeping with state laws.

c. Recognizes the limits of sole-possession records and understands these records are a memory aid for the creator and in absence of privilege communication may be subpoenaed and may become educational records when they (1) are shared with others in verbal or written form, (2) include information other than professional opinion or personal observations, and/or (3) are made accessible to others.

d. Establishes a reasonable timeline for purging sole-possession records or case notes. Suggested guidelines include shredding sole-possession records when the student transitions to the next level, transfers to another school, or graduates. Careful discretion and deliberation should be applied before destroying sole-possession records that may be needed by a court of law such as notes on child abuse, suicide, sexual harassment, or violence.

A.9. Evaluation, Assessment, and Interpretation

The professional school counselor:

a. Adheres to all professional standards regarding selecting, administering, and interpreting assessment measures and only utilizes assessment measures that are within the scope of practice for school counselors.

b. Seeks specialized training regarding the use of electronically-based testing programs in administering, scoring, and interpreting that may differ from that required in more traditional assessments.

c. Considers confidentiality issues when utilizing evaluative or assessment instruments and electronically-based programs.

d. Provides interpretation of the nature, purposes, results, and potential impact of assessment/evaluation measures in language the student(s) can understand.

e. Monitors the use of assessment results and interpretations, and takes reasonable steps to prevent others from misusing the information.

f. Uses caution when utilizing assessment techniques, making evaluations, and interpreting the performance of populations not represented in the norm group on which an instrument is standardized.

g. Assesses the effectiveness of his or her program in having an impact on students' academic, career, and personal/social development through accountability measures especially examining efforts to close achievement, opportunity, and attainment gaps.

A.10. Technology

The professional school counselor:

a. Promotes the benefits of and clarifies the limitations of various appropriate technological applications. The counselor promotes technological applications (1) that are appropriate for the student's individual needs, (2) that the student understands how to use and (3) for which follow-up counseling assistance is provided.

b. Advocates for equal access to technology for all students, especially those historically underserved.

c. Takes appropriate and reasonable measures for maintaining confidentiality of student information and educational records stored or transmitted over electronic media including although not limited to fax, electronic mail, and instant messaging.

d. While working with students on a computer or similar technology, takes reasonable and appropriate measures to protect students from objectionable and/or harmful online material.

e. Who is engaged in the delivery of services involving technologies such as the telephone, videoconferencing, and the Internet takes responsible steps to protect students and others from harm.

A.11. Student Peer Support Program

The professional school counselor:

Has unique responsibilities when working with student-assistance programs. The school counselor is responsible for the welfare of students participating in peer-to-peer programs under his or her direction.

B. RESPONSIBILITIES TO PARENTS/GUARDIANS

B.1. Parent Rights and Responsibilities

The professional school counselor:

a. Respects the rights and responsibilities of parents/guardians for their children and endeavors to establish, as appropriate, a collaborative relationship with parents/guardians to facilitate the student's maximum development.

b. Adheres to laws, local guidelines, and ethical standards of practice when assisting parents/guardians experiencing family difficulties that interfere with the student's effectiveness and welfare.

c. Respects the confidentiality of parents/guardians.

d. Is sensitive to diversity among families and recognizes that all parents/guardians, custodial and noncustodial, are vested with certain rights and responsibilities for the welfare of their children by virtue of their role and according to law.

B.2. Parents/Guardians and Confidentiality

The professional school counselor:

a. Informs parents/guardians of the counselor's role with emphasis on the confidential nature of the counseling relationship between the counselor and student.

b. Recognizes that working with minors in a school setting may require counselors to collaborate with students' parents/guardians.

c. Provides parents/guardians with accurate, comprehensive, and relevant information in an objective and caring manner, as is appropriate and consistent with ethical responsibilities to the student.

d. Makes reasonable efforts to honor the wishes of parents/guardians concerning information regarding the student, and in cases of divorce or separation exercises a good-faith effort to keep both parents informed with regard to critical information with the exception of a court order.

C. RESPONSIBILITIES TO COLLEAGUES AND PROFESSIONAL ASSOCIATES

C.1. Professional Relationships

The professional school counselor:

a. Establishes and maintains professional relationships with faculty, staff, and administration to facilitate an optimum counseling program.

b. Treats colleagues with professional respect, courtesy, and fairness. The qualifications, views, and findings of colleagues are represented to accurately reflect the image of competent professionals.

c. Is aware of and utilizes related professionals, organizations, and other resources to whom the student may be referred.

C.2. Sharing Information With Other Professionals

The professional school counselor:

a. Promotes awareness and adherence to appropriate guidelines regarding confidentiality, the distinction between public and private information and staff consultation.

b. Provides professional personnel with accurate, objective, concise, and meaningful data necessary to adequately evaluate, counsel, and assist the student.

c. If a student is receiving services from another counselor or other mental health professional, the counselor, with student and/or parent/guardian consent, will inform the other professional and develop clear agreements to avoid confusion and conflict for the student.

d. Is knowledgeable about release of information and parental rights in sharing information.

D. RESPONSIBILITIES TO THE SCHOOL AND COMMUNITY

D.1. Responsibilities to the School

The professional school counselor:

a. Supports and protects the educational program against any infringement not in student's best interest.

b. Informs appropriate officials in accordance with school policy of conditions that may be potentially disruptive or damaging to the school's mission, personnel, and property while honoring the confidentiality between the student and counselor.

c. Is knowledgeable and supportive of the school's mission and connects his or her program to the school's mission.

d. Delineates and promotes the counselor's role and function in meeting the needs of those served. Counselors will notify appropriate officials of conditions that may limit or curtail their effectiveness in providing programs and services.

e. Accepts employment only for positions for which he or she is qualified by education, training, supervised experience, state and national professional credentials, and appropriate professional experience.

f. Advocates that administrators hire only qualified and competent individuals for professional counseling positions.

g. Assists in developing: (1) curricular and environmental conditions appropriate for the school and community, (2) educational procedures and programs to meet students' developmental needs and (3) a systematic evaluation process for comprehensive, developmental, standards-based school counseling programs, services, and personnel. The counselor is guided by the findings of the evaluation data in planning programs and services.

D.2. Responsibility to the Community

The professional school counselor:

a. Collaborates with agencies, organizations and individuals in the community in the best interest of students and without regard to personal reward or remuneration.

b. Extends his or her influence and opportunity to deliver a comprehensive school counseling program to all students by collaborating with community resources for student success.

E. RESPONSIBILITIES TO SELF

E.1. Professional Competence

The professional school counselor:

a. Functions within the boundaries of individual professional competence and accepts responsibility for the consequences of his or her actions.

b. Monitors personal well-being and effectiveness and does not participate in any activity that may lead to inadequate professional services or harm to a student.

c. Strives through personal initiative to maintain professional competence including technological literacy and to keep abreast of professional information. Professional and personal growth are ongoing throughout the counselor's career.

E.2. Diversity

The professional school counselor:

a. Affirms the diversity of students, staff, and families.

b. Expands and develops awareness of his or her own attitudes and beliefs affecting cultural values and biases and strives to attain cultural competence.

c. Possesses knowledge and understanding about how oppression, racism, discrimination, and stereotyping affects her or him personally and professionally.

d. Acquires educational, consultation, and training experiences to improve awareness, knowledge, skills, and effectiveness in working with diverse populations: ethnic/racial status, age, economic status, special needs, ESL or ELL, immigration status, sexual orientation, gender, gender identity/expression, family type, religious/spiritual identity, and appearance.

F. RESPONSIBILITIES TO THE PROFESSION

F.1. Professionalism

The professional school counselor:

a. Accepts the policies and procedures for handling ethical violations as a result of maintaining membership in the American School Counselor Association.

b. Conducts herself or himself in such a manner as to advance individual ethical practice and the profession.

c. Conducts appropriate research and reports findings in a manner consistent with acceptable educational and psychological research practices. The counselor advocates for the protection of the individual student's identity when using data for research or program planning.

d. Adheres to ethical standards of the profession, other official policy statements, such as ASCA's position statements, role statement, and the ASCA National Model, and relevant statutes established by federal, state and local governments, and when these are in conflict works responsibly for change.

e. Clearly distinguishes between statements and actions made as a private individual and those made as a representative of the school counseling profession.

f. Does not use his or her professional position to recruit or gain clients, consultees for his or her private practice or to seek and receive unjustified personal gains, unfair advantage, inappropriate relationships, or unearned goods or services.

F.2. Contribution to the Profession

The professional school counselor:

a. Actively participates in local, state, and national associations fostering the development and improvement of school counseling.

b. Contributes to the development of the profession through the sharing of skills, ideas, and expertise with colleagues.

c. Provides support and mentoring to novice professionals.

G. Maintenance of Standards

Ethical behavior among professional school counselors, association members and nonmembers, is expected at all times. When there exists serious doubt as to the ethical behavior of colleagues or if counselors are forced to work in situations or abide by policies that do not reflect the standards as outlined in these Ethical Standards for School Counselors, the counselor is obligated to take appropriate action to rectify the condition. The following procedure may serve as a guide:

1. The counselor should consult confidentially with a professional colleague to discuss the nature of a complaint to see if the professional colleague views the situation as an ethical violation.

2. When feasible, the counselor should directly approach the colleague whose behavior is in question to discuss the complaint and seek resolution.

3. If resolution is not forthcoming at the personal level, the counselor shall utilize the channels established within the school, school district, the state school counseling association, and ASCA's Ethics Committee.

4. If the matter still remains unresolved, referral for review and appropriate action should be made to the Ethics Committees in the following sequence:
   - state school counselor association
   - American School Counselor Association

5. The ASCA Ethics Committee is responsible for:
   - educating and consulting with the membership regarding ethical standards.
   - periodically reviewing and recommending changes in code.
   - receiving and processing questions to clarify the application of such standards; questions must be submitted in writing to the ASCA Ethics chair.
   - handling complaints of alleged violations of the ethical standards. At the national level, complaints should be submitted in writing to the ASCA Ethics Committee, c/o the Executive Director.

SOURCE: American School Counselor Association. Used with permission.

References

Berg, I. K. (1992). Miracle picture: A vision of solutions in couple therapy. In syllabus materials for the *Special problems in marital and couples therapy: Dealing effectively with difficult couples conference.* Portola Valley, CA: Institute for the Advancement of Human Behavior.

Berg, I. K. (1994). Family-based services: A solution-focused approach. New York: W. W. Norton.

Berg, I. K., & Miller, S. D. (1992). *Working with the problem drinker: A solution-focused approach.* New York: W. W. Norton.

Cade, B., & O'Hanlon, W. H. (1993). *A brief guide to brief therapy.* New York: W. W. Norton.

Chi, M. T. H., Feltovich, P. J., & Glaser, R. (1981). Categorization and representation of physics problems by experts and novices. *Cognitive Science, 5,* 121–152.

De Jong, P., & Berg, I. K. (1998*). Interviewing for solutions.* Pacific Grove, CA: Brooks-Cole.

De Jong, P., & Miller, S. D. (1995). How to interview for client's strengths. *Social Work, 40* (6), 729–736.

de Shazer, S. (1985). *Keys to solution in brief therapy.* New York: W. W. Norton.

de Shazer, S. (1988). *Clues! Investigating solutions in brief therapy.* New York: W. W. Norton.

Durrant, M. (1995). Creative strategies for school problems: Solutions for psychologists and teachers. New York: W. W. Norton.

George, E., Iveson, C., & Ratner, H. (1999). *Problem to solution: Brief therapy with individuals and families.* London: BT Press.

Goldenberg, L., & Goldenberg, H., (2000). *Family therapy: An overview* (4th ed.). Monterey, CA: Brooks-Cole.

Irving, J. A., & Williams, D. I. (1995). Critical thinking and reflective practice in counselling. *British Journal of Guidance & Counselling, 23* (1), 107–116.

Littrell, J. (1998). *Brief counseling in action.* New York: W. W. Norton.

Metcalf, L. (1995). *Counseling toward solutions.* New York: The Center for Applied Research in Education.

Nelson, M. L., & Neufeldt, S. A. (1998). The pedagogy of counseling: A critical examination. *Counselor Education and Supervision, 38,* 70–88.

Nunnally, E. (1993). Solution focused therapy. In R. A. Wells & V. J. Giannetti (Eds.), *Casebook of the brief psychotherapies* (pp. 271–286). New York: Plenum.

O'Connell, B. (1998). *Solution-focused therapy.* Thousand Oaks, CA: Sage Publications.

O'Hanlon, W. H., & Weiner-Davis, M. (1989). *In search of solutions: A new direction in psychotherapy*. New York: W. W. Norton.

Pepinsky, J. B., & Pepinsky, N. (1954). Counseling theory and practice. New York: Ronald Press.

Prochaska, J. O., & Norcross, J. C. (1994). *Systems of psychotherapy: A transtheoretical approach*. Pacific Grove, CA: Brooks-Cole.

Ridley, C. R. (1995). *Overcoming unintentional racism in counseling and therapy: A practitioner's guide to intentional intervention*. Thousand Oaks, CA: Sage Publications.

Sklare, G. (1997). *Brief counseling works: A solution-focused approach for school counselors*. Thousand Oaks, CA: Corwin.

Tremmel, R. (1993). Zen and the art of reflective practice in teacher education. *Harvard Educational Review, 63* (4), 434–460.

Walter, J. L., & Peller, J. E. (1992). *Becoming solution-focused in brief therapy*. New York: Brunner/Mazel.

Watts, R. E., & Pietrzak, D. (2000). Adlerian "encouragement" and the therapeutic process of solution-focused brief therapy. *Journal of Counseling & Development, 78*, 442–447.

White, M., & Epston, D. (1990). *Narrative means to a therapeutic ends*. New York: W. W. Norton.

Index

CORWIN
A SAGE Company

The Corwin logo—a raven striding across an open book—represents the union of courage and learning. Corwin is committed to improving education for all learners by publishing books and other professional development resources for those serving the field of PreK–12 education. By providing practical, hands-on materials, Corwin continues to carry out the promise of its motto: **"Helping Educators Do Their Work Better."**